POETRY NOW

STAND UP POETS

Edited by Andrew Head

First published in Great Britain in 1996 by
POETRY NOW
1-2 Wainman Road, Woodston,
Peterborough, PE2 7BU

HB ISBN 1 86188 436 2
SB ISBN 1 86188 431 1

FOREWORD

Although we are a nation of poetry writers we are accused of not reading poetry and not buying poetry books: after many years of listening to the incessant gripes of poetry publishers, I can only assume that the books they publish, in general, are books that most people do not want to read.

Poetry should not be obscure, introverted, and as cryptic as a crossword puzzle: it is the poet's duty to reach out and embrace the world.

The world owes the poet nothing and we should not be expected to dig and delve into a rambling discourse searching for some inner meaning.

The reason we write poetry (and almost all of us do) is because we want to communicate: an ideal; an idea; or a specific feeling. Poetry is as essential in communication, as a letter; a radio; a telephone, and the main criteria for selecting the poems in this anthology is very simple: they communicate.

Faced with hundreds of poems and a limited amount of space, the task of choosing the final poems was difficult and as editor one tries to be as detached as possible (quite often editors can become a barrier in the writer-reader exchange) acting as go between, making the connection, not censoring because of personal taste.

Stand Up Poets is a truly uplifting publication full to the brim with humorous poems. People from all walks of life have come together with the intention of bringing a smile to readers' faces. And what better way to express our thoughts than through humour?

So if you're feeling down in the dumps and need a pick-me-up, pick up this book and be prepared to laugh at the rib-tickling poems inside! After all they say that laughter is the best medicine . . .

The success of this collection, and all previous *Poetry Now* anthologies, relies on the fact that there are as many individual readers as there are writers.

CONTENTS

CAT-TEASE

My cat's got fleas!
I'm afraid it's the truth:
She scratches daily,
While they exercise, with ease.
When I reach out
for the Exorcism spray,
To knock them down:
She runs away!
Perhaps my cat
Loves to play
with fleas.

Martina Peters

WIFE ON HOLIDAY

I have his presence every passing hour:
made fast and cabin'd, marriage has turned sour.
He in his glory deftly helms the boat:
I, press-ganged crew, may soon tear out his throat.

The foredeck's sloping: how can ageing, I,
never a shellback, nervous, far from spry,
captive and sworn at on this wretched hoy,
ever quite count on picking up the buoy.

He barring August is at work all day:
I have my own life, we are both OK.
I'm cold, calloused, rope-burnt, wind-burnt, seasick, numb.
Oh please dear God soon let September come.

P S Joll

OUCH

My friend Tom the silly prick
By the bath burnt his dick
Karron laughed howled and screamed
To see it shrink by the steam
A touch brings it to attention.
Now all it needs is an extension.
It can't be said and never should
Hot water does no good.
He's washed his lower parts it seems.
Now he's letting off some steam.
So if a bath you take make sure it's cool
For heaven's sake or just like Tom you'll
Shrink the thing and end up
With a finger for your pinky ring

B Baxter

YOU'RE HAVING A LAUGH

Laugh and the world laughs with you. Tara
was doing me a perm. Rollers all done. But
alas it was time to run. Clock said ten. Work
done. Pick up son Jamie. Looked a sight in
the night. Enough to give anyone a fright.
Hats didn't fit. Scarf will do. I wish I
had car windows you couldn't see through.
Rainy night. Jamie and John rang.
In my night dress gaily sang. Had to
run time short. Hope car doesn't stop
Picked them up. What a laugh made
it home to have my bath.

Catherine Stanton

UNTITLED

Time for my check-up, I've not slept all night,
my stomach is churning, I'm frozen with fright.
Brush round the corners, floss round the bends,
now just cross my fingers and see what God sends.

Here comes the postman, what did he say,
'Glorious morning, have a nice day!'
Get a clean hanky, don't close the door,
pop to the toilet, just once more.

Off down the pavement, oh I'm running quite fast,
was that my husband I have just passed?
Turn at the cross-roads, first on the right,
the dentist's sign is coming in sight.

The walls are vibrating, what is that din,
I'll pop in the toilet before I go in.
'You're next, Mrs Throttle, take a seat by the door'
I'm now feeling rigid, my feet stuck to the floor.

Flat on my back, my mouth open wide
with spikes and mirrors and dentist inside.
'Well, Mrs Throttle, everything's fine,
pay at the desk and I'll see you next time.'

With shaking hand I sign my cheque,
another appointment, Oh yes what the heck.
'Can you come in December at half-past three?'
'Oh that will be fine, I am sure I am free.'

Out on the pavement, a smile on my face,
I stroll down the road at a leisurely pace.
I'll stop at the sweet shop for a large chocolate bar,
now hold in a minute, did I come in the car?

Valerie Duffy

HOORAY FOR CAMELOT

It wasn't the stains on his collar, or the long blonde hairs on his cuff,
It wasn't the smell of her perfume, though,
Lord knows, I've smelt it enough.
It wasn't his late work excuses, or, the company weekend conventions,
I figured it out, years ago, about the
Bit on the side intentions!

My suitcase is packed and waiting,
A letter is stood on the shelf,
There's a Camelot cheque in my pocket,
From now on I'll please myself.

I'm happy as O'Reilly, Bahamas here I come,
I'm off to enjoy every penny,
Of this million pounds I've won.

Goodbye to being a doormat,
Farewell selfish man -
Any regrets about leaving?
'Nar' - I don't give a damn.

Catherine Whyley

TALENT

I should have been a singer
Oh I'd really love to croon
I should have been a singer
But I just can't keep in tune.

I should have been a dancer
'Cause I love a rhythmic beat
I should have been a dancer
But I was born with two left feet.

I should have been a musician
Playing music that Beethoven wrote
I should have been a musician
But I just can't play a note.

Now I can't sing and I can't dance
And playing music is not for me
So how did I manage to produce a child
Who can damn well do all three?

Angela Green

DAY AT THE FUN FAIR

Heading for the dodgems
Cars coming to me from every direction,
So I try to give it a bash
and end up with whiplash,

Struggling over to the waltzer
spinning me round and round,
Faster and faster,
When I'm finally back on the ground
it's like I'm still spinning and never stops,
All of a sudden I just drop.

Recovering an hour later it's onto the big wheel,
Taking me higher and higher
I can see so far afield,
Oh no I yelled when it broke down
I'd rather be back on the ground
because it just started pouring with rain
dripping wet, I certainly won't go on that again.

And they call it a Fun Fair,
it'll be a while before I go back there.

Colette Mary Child

A MIXED UP LAUGH

Once, and some time back, there were two cinemas facing each other
A woman went for a job, and was interviewed by the manager
The interview went well, she was told to start work on the
following Monday afternoon
The weekend went by, the time to start work came too soon

Not thinking she went into the cinema, the manager said, 'I
don't recall interviewing you'

But put this uniform on please do'
She started to escort people to their seats comfortably
Too busy to notice what film was showing, and too busy to see

Suddenly she noticed the Knights of the Round Table was on the screen
'Oh' she thought The Sound of Music in this cinema should have been seen
She looked out of the window, The Sound of Music was showing at
he opposite picture hall
She went red and murmured to herself, 'I feel such a fool'

What shall I do, *the afternoon and early evening came at last*
She just wished it was the last week past
'I won't go back here anymore, I cannot face this anymore.
I shall go back to the right cinema, where I should have started before.'

She then went to the manager, and stammered out the story
He kindly told her to come back to his cinema, and to let things be,

As she walked out of the cinema, her head looking down
She just couldn't look opposite, and felt like a clown

But opposite The Sound of Music was written boldly from the other
cinema hall
The sound just rang in her ears, she felt just like Lucille Ball

But homeward bound she went through the clear moonlight
Making up her mind to go back to The Knights of the Round Table
even through this mixed up sight
Still feeling embarrassed about the cinema opposite
But the woman was myself, no other could get mixed up like this.

Jean McGovern

COMEDY TONIC

How long since a hardy laugh . . .
It was last night, comedy tonic,
After the opening of the meeting,
And usual greetings!

The secretary got up to tell us of what was in hand,
Within half an hour none of us could understand,
She is one who teaches writing to the mental infirm,
Last night believe it or not . . . was our turn!

She did us good, well and true . . .
Stating we should buy a page in the local rag,
To explain our intentions, of what we can do,
Talk about comedy cost, we thought she was lost.

The thing she did not know about was that . . .
The depty chairlady is a graduate of university,
Speaking five languages, when told . . .
Her teeth fell out, comedy tonic was about!

All the people became crossed legged . . .
Eyes full of tears and mighty floods,
Because she thought she had a class of kids,
It was dreadful trying our laughter to control,
'Where's me teeth . . . ?' Poor old sole!

Anita Slattery

PATIENCE

It is four o'clock
The light is fading
Beneath my chair
The cat is stirring.

Can he really
Know the timing
Of the food
He is expecting?

All day he sleeps
Without a stir
Curled in oblivion
His ball-like fur.

But now it seems
His instincts say
That five o'clock
Is on the way.

A throaty meow
Comes now and then
Its urgent message
When oh! When.

A clatter of
The plate and tin
Gives hope and joy
To such as him.

At last the food
Is placed before
That black furred
Monster we adore.

Pauline Bunkin

NIGHT SCRAWLER

I'm not an intellectual, I work on
the building site.
I toil from early morning, till I
get home at night. Me hands are
hard and callused, me face as
tough as leather, me back is crook
from years and years of grafting
out in the weather.

I never went to night school,
in fact I seldom went to day.
The informative years I preferred
to spend just going out to play.

I love to write in verse, though me
spelling's quite atrocious,
but with dictionary in hand, I
can sound somewhat precocious.

I send me lyrics off to mags, to see
if they will print 'em,
and get a thrill when they say they
will, 'cos it seems as if I've
fooled 'em.

For I'm not an intellectual, nor a
poet, or too bright.
I'm just a scrawler off the building
site, when I get home at night.

T S Hurford

FISHING FABLE

At the start of the coarse season,
keen fisher persons,
adept with their lines,
spring clean their tackle,
dust down their flies.

Prepare to scatter the cloud bait wide
paint the hooks with *rouge noir.*
Pray for a good catch,
and the skill to land it.

Then when the rod tip bends
and the float *takes a dive,*
suddenly you're hooked and
slipping . . . sliding
into black fishnet.

David Robinson

BAD LUCK

I bumped my head,
Then I felt dizzy,
I fell out the door,
I am in a tizzy.
I slipped in a field
There was mud everywhere,
I trod on my toe,
I was full of despair.
I tripped on a log,
And I hurt my knee.
Why do bad things always
happen to me?

Katie Smith (13)

CINDERELLA

I was asked to write the script
For the pantomime Cinderella.
They wanted plenty of comedy lines
For the gals and the fellas.
The ugly sisters, as you would guess,
Were a great inspiration,
And the lines I gave them
Turned out to be the best.
Where have men's braces got to?
The stout one said in sorrow.
The thin one said, even more sadly,
Where have men, that's what I want to know!
The stout one said, am I too old.
Is my youth behind me now?
The thin one looked at her,
The protruding bottom as she sat,
That's where your youth and past has gone,
Behind you - what man would fancy *that!*
At least, I'm thin, with still a figure.
You, you make the audience snigger!
The fellas got a laugh or two,
But after they accused me
Of pandering to the gals too much.
Well, they were beautiful - wouldn't you?
The sell-out crowd went home happy,
And that made me happy too.
It's laughter that keeps us going,
Through and through.

Raymond Paul Kirby

DREAMING

With the outer gate shut,
I survey my estate:
Flowers, shrubs and grass
All look just great!
No weeds on the path,
As I approach my house;
The paint fresh and bright,
And no sign of that mouse!
I open the door,
Wipe my feet on the mat;
Hang up my coat,
Right next to my hat.
Everything neat,
Not a crumb on the floor;
My clothes washed and ironed,
Packed away, in the drawer.
Pull wide open the curtains,
To look at the shore:
There are boats on the river;
It's not cold, any more.
A lottery loafer,
With no shortage of cash.
Buy what I like:
No more bangers and mash!
Holiday in the Tropics,
Sun, hot as the brochure said.
Think I've died, and gone to Heaven,
Lying on a sunbed!
You run up from the shoreline,
Drop water, on my sleepy head . . .
Wake, to find the rain has come:
It's soaked me, in my bed!

Put a bowl upon the pillow,
Hope it catches all the drips;
Then rush out the door, for the early shift:
Ain't life just a bitch?

Richard A Peters

I SHOULD HAVE KNOWN

Oh dear! Oh Lord! This cannot be
My husband making cups of tea
He's mowed the lawn, and made the bed
(Quite well too, it must be said)
He's fed the cat and changed her tray
Not a nice job, I can say.

He's chopped the onions with some tears
And done jobs he's put off for years
'Sit down love'. He told me.
'I'll go and make a cup of tea.'
What another one, I nearly said
But put my feet up instead!

What a lovely man, how he's changed
My opinion of him rearranged
But wait a minute, I should have known
Forest football team are playing at home!

The poor man can't go, he hurt his head
He's had to go and lie down instead
The bump's quite big I must say
- He walked into a cat litter tray!

Anne Greatorex

AB-SOLUTION

The ozone is, as we all know
The fresh air at the seaside.
But lead and fluorocarbons flow
Upward. Destruction world-wide!

To work for years we went our way
On two boiled eggs with gusto.
But now eggs make us ill they say.
Eat muesli, bran and nutso.

Ration your drink. You dare no smoke,
Rain forests are a-tumbling.
And if with butter toast I spread -
You'll kill yourself, they're rumbling.

Now here we sit. His eyes meet mine,
My grandson is the future.
The world one day I'll leave to him.
He'll win - with Mother Nature.

Roma Scrivener

BLOOMING BIRDS

It was very funny.
The people's faces shown
a look of pure amazement,
as all the birds came down.

The lady she was waiting,
there to catch the bus.
The pigeons flew right on her,
She really made a fuss.

One nearly landed on her head.
But, she brushed it away.
They were there to get the bread,
that on the floor did lay.

Her black coat now had mess on.
Her hair was out of place.
The day the pigeons cam down.
and the lady lost her grace.

Linda Gillard

MOTHER'S DAY

Say 'Hello' to Mothers' Day, my cup of joy was full
My daughter took me out to lunch, my time was far from dull
I taxied to the restaurant, agog with thoughts so grand
I felt more full of happiness than any in the land
My daughter looked a picture, but I felt I could compete
Although, when on comparing, not so hot around the feet
My days of high stiletto heels are gone beyond recall
I have to stick to flatties, just in case I have a fall
I ate through several courses, and I drank a lot of wine
My confidence was sky high, and I felt the world was mine
The waiter was obsequious, admiring me, I thought
But then there was a happening, though nothing I had sought
He proffered me a present, which I took with slight amaze
I think the quantity of wine somehow put me in a daze
Annoyed I felt, humiliated, for I thought he oughter
At least have queried which was mother, and therefore which was daughter!

Doris Holland

RADICAL POETRY

Celery and tomatoes.
My mind is going round.
Do I really need a lover?
Fantasies are wonderful . . .
reality is hard work!
My bones are getting creaky.
'Woman seeks man for company and fun.'
Flirting and lusting . . . is all in the mind.
Sex is hard work -
from a practical aspect!
As I go batty.
. . . jog with me.
My kids say . . . mum's gone round the twist . . .
. . . just a bit.
Eccentric . . . is how I would describe her!
Must be the menopause.
Don't forget the URC Party.
Celery and tomatoes . . . for our Dear Minister.
Boxed packed . . . the office is moving house.
As the new year comes around . . .
Mulled wine and mince pies . . . coming out of my ears.
Christmas carols . . . go round in my mind.
A lover for Christmas is what I want.
So, as I go, just slightly batty . . . Helen
Get me an advocate . . . to keep me on the
Straight and narrow.
The tree of knowledge brought tears for Adam and Eve.
The Garden of Paradise is where I want to be!
For God only knows what's going on inside my
Head!

Attilia Padden

A GIANT WORLD

The world is a giant,
That is asleep.
When the clouds come over,
He's under a sheet.

It starts to rain,
It starts to pour,
The giant has wet his bed
Once more.

The trees are his hairs,
We're shaving them off.
When the wind blows,
He's having a cough.

We're infesting his body,
For we are bugs.
We're spreading infection,
Not lovingly hugs.

When the world,
Goes round the sun.
The giant is dancing,
And burning his bum.

A volcano is a spot,
Which the giant has squeezed.
And the lava like puss,
Flows out with ease.

We know why we live
On the giant earth.
We're here to bug and dirty him,
And we're wasting more time than it's worth.

Sara Morgan

I WISH I WAS

I wish I was,
Just because,
It would be so nice,
I could eat a slice.

I wish I was,
Really I do,
To be free to be me,
To do.

I wish I was,
Like I said before,
Feel like snow,
You will never know,
What I wished for!

Karl Phillipson

THE MONDAY BLUES

Monday has started again without me.
There are cars outside roaring by.
It's passed nine o'clock, but I'm not getting up,
Although I know soon - I must try.

The postman's delivered the mail for this morning
There's plenty of bills I am sure
Charities asking for help with the homeless
            The hungry, infirm and the poor.

I don't possess much for myself and the family
And all of this causes such stress
I'll just 'Soldier on' and tackle the work load
To get myself out of this mess.

Thelma J Town-Clear

A COLD

I've started with this flaming cold, I've a tap inside my head
        Someone seems to turn it on every time I go to bed,
I think I need a plumber to stop this awful flow
        I don't need a light as my nose is all aglow.

I need a hot water bottle as I'm all a shiver
        Just like a chicken with a frozen liver,
Now I feel too hot and there's water on my knees
        Atishoo, atishoo another bloomin sneeze.

I have a musical bug playing a loud refrain
        Dancing with his boots on inside my brain,
My throat hurts so much I can't even drink
        It's lined with sandpaper instead of mink.

My eyes are full of water, its running down my cheeks
        I think I need an overhaul I have so many leaks,
My lips are swollen and covered in cold sores
        No one will want to kiss me, with ugly open pores.

Now I am off to bed, every step will make me moan
        I am only half way up and there goes the flippin phone,
With a squeaky voice I answer, the caller is dismayed
        He thought he'd phoned to China, at least that's what he said.

I rub myself with vicks and smell like a chemist shop
        My partner turned his back on me, I am an awful flop,
I'll cry myself to sleep, I wont even get a hug
        My partner doesn't want me, he doesn't want my bug.

Christine Farquhar

WALKING MUMS

It was on my mother's seventieth birthday
She announced she would walk two miles a day
She said she was going to make herself fit
And thought walking would be a good way

After walking fourteen miles on the first week
She said she had twinges in her knees
But she hoped, as the time went by
The pains would gradually ease.

And so she went into her second week
On her first week she just managed to toddle
But now she says she is into her stride
And finds walking becoming a doddle

She told me her skin is becoming quite tanned
And her hair bleached gold by the sun
She said she had never ever realised
That walking could be so much fun

She told me of the nice people
She meets, as she goes on her way
And she is glad she took up walking
She really does bless the day

I thought she was passed it at seventy
But one thing, I have found
At two miles a day for nearly a year
She really has covered some ground

It's her seventy first birthday next Tuesday
I would love to send her flowers and a card
But I don't know where the devil she is
Finding her is proving real hard.

Frederick Sowden

MY NEW TEETH

At the Castle-gate market - I spied some false teeth
Says I 'Man- they look braw!'
So I gave the man a tanner for them
And went hame tae show my Ma!

I wore them to the club that night
I would impress my chums.
Then some-one slapped me on the back
And they landed in Kathy's rum!

Man! I was fairly mortified!
In tears for all to see.
Whilst my poor teeth lay in that rum
Just smiling up at me!

Betty and Helen were in stitches!
Grunting like twa pigs.
And I was sore affronted
So! I dug them in the ribs!

Marje and Jean were just as bad.
Rolling about in fits.
'Cause I couldna eat my tattie crisps
Could just sook little bits!

Kathy just sat and stared at me.
In truth! She couldna speak.
The poor quine hasna' recovered yet,
She's been aff her rum for weeks!

Still! I never lose my teeth now.
They just bide in my mou!
Nae mair divin' in tae rum
They're stuck fast wi super glue!

Lily T Ross

BLACK WIDOW'S SONG

It could be said, I'm always left on the shelf
After they've stuffed me, I've always stuffed myself
So girls listen now, listen to my advice
No matter what they say, love never cums twice
And to avoid heartburn it is a good bet
To strike before the post-coital cigarette
And I remember the first time, my first mate
I suppose you gotta put it down to fate
He leapt upon me, really quite unafraid
And, gosh! Oh boy! was he dying to get laid
Was the tastiest guy that I ever ate
There were no leavings on the side of my plate
There was one guy, I just knew would be such fun
I got a gut feeling about this one
Said he was on holiday, came from Cadiz
Was so well hung, from my silken threads that is
So! some have been low-lifes, you might say the dregs
So hey! come on now! are you pulling my legs?
What do I think of, each time I am a bride?
It's very, very simple, 'Baked, boiled or fried?'
They've gotta take me for better or for worse
But they should, first, think to order up a hearse
Not much into legs, they gaze into my eyes
The last things they see before their demise
Some have been fat, others skinny as a peg
After all, a leg, is a leg, is a leg!
This rich source of protein to which I am prone
Ensures that I never, ever dine alone
I am told the day will come and I'll rue
All the past lovers I've munched my way through
If I had my life, to live it all again
I'd do it all just the same, cos I ate men!

P Murrum

DREADFUL AFTERNOON

Waiting for an engineer to come,
to rectify a 'Wash and dry' machine,
With constant speculation centred on
returning to, 'an everyday routine'
when the telephone is urgent, on the
silence, and my twin brother's son
speaks words of dread, to tell me,
almost in a single sentence,
that his father, and my much loved twin
is dead.

Grey stone walls cast shadow shapes on pavements,
providing cool and shade for autumn days,
where cars are parked in lines, of dumb bereavement,
as breezes tease the leaves of sad bouquets
providing such a brilliant splash of colours,
in line along the edges of the drive,
as we stand here, with brimming eyes, perceiving,
a loved one gone, whilst we remain alive.

Momentary gathered, close relations,
united, in a family, to mourn,
remembering, close varied situations
With their ever changing character and form,
but sharing their regretting at the parting,
of someone, 'took for granted' recently,
but now aware, as brimming eyes are smarting.
and prayer-book words, are difficult to see.

Walter Gilder

THOMAS

My son Thomas what will I do
With a mucky little fella like you
You go out to play all fresh and clean
Then when you get back what a scene.

You said you were Tarzan and climbed the trees
No wonder there's a great big hole in your knee
But you're covered in mud where has it come from
'Oh I was a soldier and I planted a bomb.

You go round the farm but you can't stay away
From the smelly old cow and the barn full of hay
You come back home a tired and happy lad
But your sisters all run cause you smell so bad.

Well into the bath let's get you clean
Can I be a sailor and play submarines
I know what will happen can you guess
The floor will be awash oh what a mess

But now it's time for you to sleep
And quietly into your bed you creep
The day is over thank goodness says me
Now all I need is a strong cup of tea.

Christine Spurrell

RUBBER BANDS

Rubber bands are good to use.
For pinging across the classroom.
For pinging on our hands.
For pinging messages to our best mate.

You can cut them with scissors.
You can cut them with a knife.
The only problem with rubber bands
is . . . *They get you into . . .*
Strife!

Emma-Dawn Loftus

UNDER PRESSURE

I was in the conservatory oblivious to all
Watching our rabbit playing with a ball
When suddenly after a hiss and a bang
Into the kitchen I ran
Whereupon I saw my spouse
Green and foaming at the mouth
You stupid woman he spluttered in rage
Suddenly looking his age
There were peas on the ceiling and the floor
Up the walls above the door
My husband had them on his glasses and in his hair
There were mushy peas everywhere
The pressure cooker had exploded
When the washer had corroded
But it seemed it was my fault
Or so my husband thought
And as I stood in front of my bloke
I couldn't help but see the joke
Him so serious covered in peas
Then he began to sneeze
My daughters and I collapsed in laughter
As he told of his premonition of the hereafter
'I could have had a heart attack' he said
'I could have been dead'
As another pea slipped down his nose
That's what being under pressure means I suppose.

Jean Martin

WHODUNNIT?

When old Humpty Dumpty was sat on his wall
Just what was it caused him to have a great fall?
Perhaps the Old Woman who lived in a shoe
Tripped over and nudged him after having a few!
What about the blind mice? Couldn't see where they're going,
They could have knocked him without ever knowing!
Hey diddle-diddle, while playing his fiddle
Was the cat sure of which way to go?
With his brain in the middle of solving the riddle
Did he knock Humpty off with his bow?
Little Bo-peep had lost her sheep,
The poor girl had started to cry.
Sense couldn't keep as she started to weep,
One prod with her crook and goodbye!
Mary Mary, she's contrary, always one for a fight,
Did she go to the wall for no reason at all
And push Dumpty off out of spite?

So why did he fall? We've never been told,
Just that poor old Humpty would never grow old;
Call it old age, or a sign of the times
But I've lost all faith in our Nursery Rhymes!

Robbie

WHISKERS

Whiskers quivering just a bit
Help me sense if I can fit
Into the opening that seems to me
So very small beneath this tree.
Kneading digging, this is fun
(Enough of sleeping in the sun)
Reaching scratching - still no luck
Squeezing pushing - gosh, I'm *Stuck!*

Danatt Robert Sharpe

FIRE DRILL

If you're a pretty lady,
With a figure that is nice,
I hope you will forgive me,
If I offer some advice.
These days it's not considered rude.
To go to bed completely nude.
So let the air get to your body,
By always sleeping in the noddy.

Some people pack pyjamas,
When they visit a hotel,
In case one night, they wake with fright,
And hear the fire bell,
But if you haven't got a nightie,
You need not fear the worst,
You can bet your bottom dollar,
That you'll be rescued first.

Gerry Boxall

LION BOY

There was a young boy called Ryan
who thought that he was a lion,
he roared all day
when he was out to play
and frightened his friends away,
he growled whenever he heard the 'phone
and even ate his poor dogs bone,
his family coped
by living in hope,
that one day
thesc lion thoughts would go away,
so they could live happily again.

Linda Casey

WHOSE FOOTPRINTS?

I'm in such a muddle fuddle,
I don't know what to do,
I've found this set of footprints,
And they're not from me or you.

They may belong to Jack in the box,
No he's got springs instead of legs,
I suppose they're something like a cauliflower
Or is it scrambled eggs.

All over the draining board,
And the dishes I have washed
All over the living room floor and . . .
Oh no, oh yes, oh gosh.

All along the hallway
And right the way upstairs,
I've just this minute done my chores,
But whose ever they are can't care.

My mind is in such a fluster
I pout, I moan, and grump,
And then, just look, I've got him
It was that pesky Mr Flump.

J A Glover Phillips

REAL FRUIT YOGHURT

Real fruit yoghurt's great!
You don't even need a plate.
You can eat it from the tub,
It is most nutritious grub.

And if you have to watch your waist,
You can still enjoy the taste.
As they have those low-fat versions,
For all calorie-conscious persons.

And as for real fruit flavour,
There's an extensive range to savour.
With fruit chunky bits to see,
Or alternatively . . . puree.

But there *is* one common fact,
When you buy a family pack.
Though you swoop like crazed piranha,
The slowest gets . . . banana!

George Keay

AT OUR SEASIDE

On our beach there grows sand castles with flags, families with bulging bags
Sand is kicked into every nook and cranny by excited children in charge
of Granny
Deck chairs are hired, Grandads retired, socks removed for a
sea-water soothe.
Mum decides to have a swim but is having a job to tuck it all in,
Dad is digging for hidden treasure perhaps get to Australia for good measure,
Son is pretending to have a rest, spying, with half closed lids at a
girl in a vest.
Daughter is desperate trying to get brown, with not enough protection
her defences are down
Mum has gone for a game of Bingo,
Dad deep in his hole may find a Dingo,
Grandad is eating fish and chips, he kisses Granny with his salty lips.
Son has sand between his toes, his confidence grows exchanging numbers of
The phone with vest clad girl alone.
It's started to rain, what a pain,
Gather up rush mats, the kiss me quick hats, precious shells, food that smells,
Bucket and spade, warm lemonade, empty tins that sometimes miss the bins,
Sun lotion, Grandads secret potion, a half eaten pear, Grannies false hair,
Knickers, frocks, sandy socks,
Despite all that pain they come back and do it again.

Shirley Perring

THE WATCHERS

'Pass me the TV Times, dear
And let me see what's on tonight.
Cops and robbers, it would appear,
Wrestling and the big fight.'

The heavy door shuts with a bang.
The jailer's footsteps echo away.
This prisoner was the last of the gang
That had been brought in that day.

They appeared in court the very next day
After a night in the cold cell.
They were charged with theft and causing an affray
Which the police had then to quell.

The gang, made up of three girls and a boy
Were stealing from an electrical shop
One girl then caused a scene as a ploy
When a woman suddenly cried 'Stop!'

One of the girls was caught red-handed.
The boy ran off to the street.
They were all duly reprimanded
And the police went back on the beat.

The wife yawned and said 'Cocoa, dear?
The wrestling's finished, I've no doubt.
There's nothing else to watch, I fear.
Turn off the lights and put the cat out.'

Helen Cronin

FINAL WHISTLE

The whistle blew the game had begun
He caught the ball and began to run
But he tripped over on an undone lace
And fell in the mud flat on his face

He was covered in mud from head to toe
He couldn't even see which way to go
But on being passed the ball he ran with pride
And scored a try for the other side

Being the kicker it was his role
His team having scored he had to go for goal
To kick the ball well he ran at it hard
And missed it completely, although it rolled one yard

Poor Johnny he was having such a bad day
More often than not he got in the way
At one point he was passed the ball from the scrum
He forgot what to do and was knocked on his bum

At least it looked as though he'd found his feet
He side stepped and dummied, to watch was a treat
His team at this they could not frown
Until the elastic snapped and his shorts fell down

The final whistle blew the game had to come to an end
Thought Johnny so his team he would not offend
On exchanging shirts he held his head up high
Even doing that he elbowed someone in the eye

In the changing rooms they collaborated to scheme
He thought this is it I'm out of the team
But he couldn't believe his luck at what they said
They must think highly of me, I'm to go to Coventry instead.

W Lister

IT'S A DOG'S LIFE

I was born at a very young age, ma wasn't glad she was in a rage
She wanted a budgie a dog or a cat
Looked at me and said 'I'm not having that'
My face was all wrinkled like the dark side of the moon
Ma said 'I've seen better looking prunes'
I was born in Berking and I cried and whimpered the first two days
Ma took me to the Doctor and this is what he says
There's nowt seriously wrong but it would help my friend
If you put the nappy on the right end
Just who was I like me mam or me dad
More like a Bulldog or the Elephant Man
When my dad set a lawn at the front of the house
Birds nicked the seed and dad would shout
Dad said to mam 'Can Sandra sleep in her pram outside'
The birds took one look and flew away to hide
My brother was 2+ when I was born he looked at me his face full of scorn
Said he, 'Mam', 'what! Is that, I wanted a budgie, dog or a cat.'
As I got older played outside in the yard as neighbours passed
they stared very hard
One of them stopped my mam at the shops
And said, 'What kind of dog is that you've got',
That's my daughter Sandra mam said so 'polite', and
If you don't shut up she'll give you a bite
When you're an ugly baby life's tough, so what!
But I had the last laugh and I laughed a lot
Ma entered me in Crufts, got best unknown breed
So she who laughs last laughs longest indeed
And I wear my blue ribbon for all to see
As I sniff round the bottom of my favourite tree
Mam picks me up by the scruff 'When it's time for tea
She's a pal and a chum yessiree.

Sandra Witt

DIY

Did you ever try
To paint a ceiling
Nine feet high
On your own?

Did you ever cover
A wall
Nine feet tall
With ready-pasted paper
Which refused to stick
But silently rolled itself
Into a ball
Around your head?

Did you ever find
When all was done
That the wallpaper batch
You'd chosen
Didn't match
The curtains
. . . or the carpet?

But did you ever
Reach an end,
Walls, ceiling,
Carpet, bedding
All to blend?
What sense of satisfaction
And there's money saved enough
To spend
On further
Decoration!

Dee Yates

THE WRITING CLASS'S BOOZE UP

The year is out, well almost
The book has had its launch
Now celebrate together
The class of '94
Let's have a few good bevies
A pint or two for Jack
A 'G' and 'T' for mavis
A really good old yak.
Now the booze is really flowing
And none of us are stable
The cry goes up 'where's Rhoda?'
She's there, under the table
And Joan - remember what she said
If we got drunk she'll kill us
She's dancing on the table
Displaying pink French knickers.
And Wendy, well what can I say
I thought she was so sweet
But now she's had a few I see
She's fallen off her seat
And then there's me, Miss Perfect
Quiet as a lamb
I'll tell em Teach, I really will
'I'm not as drunk
As thinkle peep I am'

Carole Jones

YES, PLEASE?

Good morning, can I help you,
what would you like to buy,
cram another cake in there?
Certainly, I'll try,
it doesn't fit? Oh that's a shame,
I'll have another go,
it doesn't matter anyway,
we're here till half past four!

A stottie sliced? Why yes of course,
you know it doesn't matter
if it lacerates my fingers, and,
it makes the slicer clatter;
what can I get you, madam,
can you leave your dog outside?
Yes, I know it's raining, but he
won't help you decide!

A fresh cream mandolin?
with the coconut, that's right,
perhaps you'd like a cream French horn,
to go with that tonight,
sorry there's no mushroom
in our steak and kidney pie,
I'll see you in the morning?
most certainly, goodbye!

Tracey Taylor

MY DOG

I would like to tell you about my dog
A skinny looking whippet
Not my choice of dog at all
He was won with a raffle ticket

My neighbour next door had a poodle
She took him for walks on the moor
But when she saw me with my skinny scrag on the lead
She didn't know me any more

My pension was small to keep us both
I decided he had to go
With a bag and a brick and a long piece of string
We down to the river did go

He licked my hand and started to whine
His eyes looked oh so sad
I hadn't the courage to pick him up
And put him in the bag

I entered him in a big race
He was next to a lady called Dove
He was going mad, fair showing off
Old Samson had fallen in love.

Halfway round the lady was leading
I thought I would die of thirst
Samson chased lady for all he was worth
God love him, he came in first

The prize was 150 quid
Oh I really did feel swell
I called in the pub for a pint of beer
And bought one for Samson as well

He did me proud at the races
Brought me money when I had none
He died of old age, but I'll never forget
The best prize that I ever won

O Powell

A MOST ESSENTIAL ACCESSORY

My most essential accessory
Must be my safety pin
When all about is falling out
It tucks things safely in
Any button is replaced by it
It always helps me win
When my essential elastic snaps
It could be construed a sin
Without my faithful accessory
No doubt I'd be run in

Though you boast about your gee-gaws
Practically next of kin
No friend on earth could hug as tight
As my fragile safety pin

My Yucca plant was falling down
I had no wire too thin
My safety pin with a smaller friend
Quite neatly staked it in
So, do not think of clever things
Like sealing wax and biscuit tin
Of micro wave and curtain rings
But just a simple safety pin.

Georgina Francis McKellar

MALE MENOPAUSE

Dad was fifty-five today,
And, he didn't look too happy.
'Retirement's only *Ten* years away,
Wouldn't *You* be feeling unhappy?'

'These aches and pains would drive you crazy,
And my hair is getting thinner!'
Mum says, 'Oh, don't be such a misery,
Be quiet and drink your dinner.'

'I'm fed up with soup, since I lost my teeth,
I'll be glad when I get my new set.'
'Oh, you'll be the cat's whiskers when you get those.
You'll look really handsome, I'll bet!'

If only he didn't get so tired,
If only he could get up and dance.
We'd all be a darned sight happier,
If given the ghost of a chance.

Yes, Dad was fifty-five today,
But, he still doesn't look too glad,
So, we sang 'Happy Birthday,' anyway,
'Cos we love our miserable Dad!

Janet Swindells

KEYMEN

The trend now for men with bunches of keys,
To let them dangle from waistbands down to their knees
You can spot them half canned at quarter to four (closing time)
Wondering which is the one that opens the door.
I saw a young man once forty-five on a ring
All from his belt did trendily swing
Fall down because he'd supped too much bevvy
Unable to rise cos his keys were too heavy.

Stan McKinney

A MIX-UP AT THE STATION

One hour, seventeen and a half minutes late
The 'turbo express' was an unfortunate name
Sat, at a deserted station, a mind drifting towards hate
As he endured the biting wind and torrential rain

Clambering aboard, muttering words of utter condemnation
He chose a window seat and scowled in anger
As, on the opposite platform, another train entered the station
'Just like policemen or buses' he cried with indignant fervour

'Tickets please' yelled a grinning man in uniform
James complained how late he would be, upon arrival in Manchester
The inspector smirked and pointed to the other platform
And a train leaving, 'That was the one you wanted sir'

'This one has a straight run through to Colchester!'

Steven J Smith

COMEDIANS

Comedians give you pleasure
Telling jokes at their leisure.
Making you laugh and at ease,
Stomach ache if you please.

Laughing fit to burst,
That is something you don't rehearse.
Wet your pants, with tears streaming.
Your dignity you try redeeming.

Now the show is over
No one in the hall is sober.
Now the comedian is thawed,
When he finally drops his drawers.

Sylvia Codd

DOG'S WORK

Dogs should all have a purpose, I have always maintained.
Not petted or vetted nor unduly reined.
With my logical mind, a dog I declared
should greet an intruder with their teeth properly bared.

There's a police dog or sheepdog or one who can guide
a blind man or woman and stay by their side,
or a dog who will rescue folks buried or lost
in earthquakes or landslides 'neath cold snow and frost.

If this is so then tell me just how,
a wee thing like you
can take over my life and dictate what I'll do?
It appears plain to me
that your sole purpose in life is to spend all your days
just pleasuring me.

Norah Roden

SAUSAGES FOR TEA

Seated at the kitchen table, my favourite it's sausages for tea
Five black and charred offerings you set in front of me
Wield my knife and fork, determined I'll not be beat
Deflected off the hardened surface, find some peas to eat
Raid the tool box for my hammer and chisel, hoping it's not too late
I bashed and chipped at those black diamonds, but only cracked the plate
Ask the wife all innocent 'How long did you leave them underneath the flaming grill'
There's only one thing left to try, I unpack the pneumatic drill
Carrots, potatoes, peas and gravy, all flying through the air
The dog darts in and laps it up, thankful for his share
The table's reduced to splinters, there's nothing left of tea
Until the dust settles, five black sausage fingers staring back at me

Paul Birkitt

SCREEN GODDESS

They said it was the pressure on her
They said she was a prima donna
She was pumped with pride and honour
Compliments bestowed upon her.
The make-up girls did her looks preen
Every night she graced our screen
Though some thought it was obscene
She was in fact the uncrowned Queen.
Fitting snugly into her role
More often than not the scene she stole
From her Co-presenters,
Each night she wore a costume new
For an appreciative audience to view
That gave an impression of stalwart beauty
Few could even hope to match,
Few guests escaped without a scratch,
For her lines she did not stumble
Though her interviewees may fumble
Not averse to a scandal
Other hosts could not hold a candle
To her orchestrated preamble
Into the annals of screen sirens
And to the pens of new Lord Byron's
These the riches richly deserved
Three seats at the 'Grand' reserved
For this purveyor of light news
Boy! she was enough to blow a fuse!

Alan Fowles

ALTERNATIVES

'Aromatherapy' they said,
'Will make you smell nice,
When in bed' -
But when I got onto a bus,
The passengers all made a fuss,
So getting off at the nearest stop,
I made my way into a shop;
The minute I went through the door,
The staff all fell down on the floor;
So, opening the windows wide,
I hurried to get back outside;
A PC came up, with a frown,
Said 'What a pong, get out of town'
Off I went, at a cracking pace,
Huffing and puffing, red in face,
Mile after mile, without a break,
Until I reached my own front gate;
Opened the door, and straight upstairs,
Flinging my clothes into the air,
Steaming bathtub rubbing and scrubbing,
Soap and flannel, what a dubbing;
Then pink and shiny, all brand new,
Came out smelling of roses, *Phew!*

Dorothy Neil

BALLPOINTS

Mr Bagshot Thunderington-Crake
Bought *two* ballpoints, by mistake,
And in the bag he'd bought them in
Took them up to bed with him.
But, after he'd turned out the lights
He heard some scuffling in the night! . . .

So, turning all the lights back on
He went to look - whereupon
Out from the bag which hid the pens
Jumped an inky troop of ten! . . .
'By God! They breed like rabbits!'
he said
. . .Then putting the light out,
He went back to bed.

Kris Dickson

A BRITISH LAMENT

Don't eat fat and don't eat butter,
Don't get excited or your heart will flutter,
Don't have an egg if its got a soft yolk,
Don't rot your teeth by drinking coke,
Don't eat sugar, don't eat bread,
Don't chew your pencil, its point is made of lead,
Don't eat chocolate and keep away from toffee,
Too much tea is bad for you, and the same applies to coffee,
Water from a bottle is supposed to be the best,
Fish from the polluted sea could be added to the rest,
But please, oh please, don't stop us eating British beef,
How can we get by with just a lettuce leaf
Or a handful of raisins and a basinful of rice.
Is that what they want us to say is very nice?
They've turned our pounds to kilos, and our ounces into grams,
Who do they think we are, a flock of silly lambs?
Our milk will be powdered next, and packed up in a tin,
Twice our men have been to war, our freedom for to win,
Who are these people who call themselves just 'they'?
Do they live in London, or is it far away?
Whatever can we do to stop this slippery slide?
Is there anyone out there now who's fighting on our side?

J Gant

SEEING IS BELIEVING

I was sitting eating dinner
When down the stairs he came
The ghost of highwayman Jack
Well I think that was his name
Down the stairs he kept coming
I could not believe the sight
Swathed in that big black cape
I was paralysed with fright
My hair stood right up on end
My eyes stood out on stalks
My mouth just opened and closed
And I dropped my knife and fork
I slowly forced myself to rise
And crept across the floor
I tripped and got there sooner
And I burst right through the door
This slammed against the wall
Then fell off its hinge
Next I broke a Chinese vase
'Cos I couldn't see through my fringe
I looked at broken glass and wood
Then looked up with surprise
My coat had fallen down the stairs
You should have heard my cries!

S Gillings

ON ROBERT BURNS

From far and near
They hold him dear
And welcome give him each New Year
With many a smile and some a tear.

In lands afar with rhyme and song
The Bard is welcomed by the throng
May it be so for ever long
We hold our Prince of Poets strong.

His worldly gift our spirits lift
Aye fond memories removed from mist
Few greater pleasures it's hard to list
This great poet Scotland's gift

J Fagan

OH TO BE SLIM!

I wish I could lose weight again
My dieting now seems in vain.
I lost two stones in 1991
Which certainly was not much fun.
How it went I have not a clue
But it took one year to do.
Sadly now I can't lose any
It's all come back like a bad penny!
Twelve stones the scales show every week
Vanished is the ten I seek.
I don't eat this and don't eat that
Oh forget it, I'll just stay *fat.*
Where are my Thornton's? What a treat!
You've eaten them - I'll have a sweet.

E Hawkins

WE LAUGHED SO MUCH

My boyfriend and I we love a good laugh
It's nearly always over something silly or daft.
Like the other day on our way to the shop
We started to laugh and couldn't stop.
Something stupid he said to me!
At the time it seemed so funny,
We got to the shop and stood outside
People looked at us as our laughter we couldn't hide
There was a great big poster over the shop window
We stood in front of it so we wasn't on show
The girls in the shop couldn't see our heads
Only the bottom of our legs
They could see we were laughing as I headed for the door
I looked at their grinning faces, but they made me laugh more
Little did we know that they started to think
That we had both been at the drink
For a minute our laughter came to an end
But not for long as we started again
We were laughing so much, we got stomach ache
If we didn't stop soon, the shop would be shut, it would be too late
We never did get in the shop that day
Still laughing so much we had to walk away.
Now every time we go in the shop, the girls all grin they haven't forgot
That day we stood laughing outside the shop.

Linda Roberts

A WRINKLY TALE

There was a lass from North Yorks,
Whose wrinkles were much in her thoughts.
She'd pondered each line
Of her facial decline
Since watching those ads on TV.

Determined she answered their call,
To combat wrinkles and all.
A battle she waged
With the signs of old age
Attacking with cleansers and creams.

Although she continued her quest,
She sadly lost some of her zest.
For deep down she knew
And the thought grew
That the age old battle she'd lose.

And then in the mirror she saw,
A frown she'd not noticed before.
She was aware
Her cosmetic affair
Had seriously damaged her fun.

There was a lass from North Yorks,
Whose wrinkles were far from her thoughts.
Her facial decline
She met with a smile
And happy she was ever after.

E D Stevenson

TWITCHING WITH LAUGHTER

When a duck says quack
I wonder what it's at
For its waddle is no doddle
Like water off its back.

Have you ever watched in winter
when the ice is frozen stiff
The slidings the tripping up
Of them trying to walk upon the stuff?

Now hens another feature
Make a silly silly noise
When they run about so much
Are they trying to catch their cluck?

Fancy arriving in an egg
And sat on like a living bed
If you're not eaten up for food
Peck yourself out and join the brood.

Then there is the pelican
If he can, I can, but really
Can any of us cram so much
So deep and fly with the stuff

Birds are funny things with
Backward pointing knees
They have so many feathers
Do you think they ever sneeze?

Sheila Heighway

A SHEPHERD'S BLUES

Now Jock McSock, was tending his flock,
Down on the farm one day.
And then he paused to have his lunch
So he sat down on the hay.

He nibbled at his ploughman's lunch,
As you would expect him to.
Then next he started on his flask
Of piping hot haggis stew.

He balanced his flask, on the edge of a cask,
But this cask was rotted through.
The flask tipped over, on to the front of his pants,
And so did the piping hot stew.

The scene that followed was mayhem
Oh! You've never seen the like
Then laugh, I thought I'd never stop
And everyone took the mike.

Well, his arms went here, his legs went there
Upon this fateful morn,
This surely must have been the day
That the highland fling was born.

Don't know about fling! But the flask was flung,
And he jumped into a pond.
To cool his stew hot navel,
And whatever else lay beyond.

Next time if passing down his way,
And Jock McSock's at lunch on the hay,
Don't ask if he's got any stew,
Else he'll chuck his lunch all over you.

Peter J Sutton

THE FEMALE FORM

How many women
Are perfectly content,
With their own
Personal predicament.
Head to toe
And in between,
How many faults
Are there to be seen.
The shape of the face,
The nose, the mouth,
Have we too much
From north to south.
Or are we well-rounded
Like the globe,
Our girth expanding
Fit to explode.
Some are top-heavy,
Some have slim legs,
Others are straight
Up and down like pegs.
Droopy posteriors,
Chunky thighs,
Double chins
Or baggy eyes.
Tall or small,
Fat or thin,
Beauty is with us all,
It comes from within.

Polly Cox

MASSAGE

I woke up this morning and shouted Hooray!
It's Thursday! It's Thursday! It's my massage day.
Entering the parlour so pleasantly warm
Where the masseur is waiting, his skills to perform,
Aromatic oils pervading the air
Expertly chosen, blended with care,
Soft music playing like gurgling streams
Soothing my mind as I drift into dreams.
I feel so relaxed the world seems unreal
No words can express the way that I feel.
Cascading waterfalls, sparkling sun,
A new day awaiting a new life begun.

Dorothy Kemp

THE LAUGHTER CLINIC

There's a 'laughter clinic'
Run by Doctor Lee
Who prescribes two jokes a day,
With every cup of tea.

It's better than a pill
For they are hard to swallow.
Shame it's in the USA
Or I'd go there tomorrow.

Here it's just placebos.
Or counselling or chores.
Occupational activities,
Do nothing more than bore.

Jill Ives

THE DRIVING INSTRUCTOR

Barry was a driving instructor
By the end of the day he wished he was a bus conductor
Steve came in for his driving test
It was his first time Barry could guess
When Steve got into the car that day
Everybody started to run away
Barry shouted slow down you fool
He wouldn't have minded but they were still in the school
But the roads Steve could not wait
And soon he caught sight of the gate
With a three point turn and a reverse
And Barry knew that there was worse
Off they shot like a light
That made Barry's hair turn pure white
Steve said sit back you're in for a treat
As they sped off down the street
Up and down the roads and hills
And Barry fetched out his pick-me-up pills
First one and then some more
In the end he had taken twenty four
Suddenly there was an almighty crash
And Barry's head he did bash
Next the ambulance came
And doctors say that Barry won't be the same
But Steve he just would not go
He said there's something I need to know
But Barry he could guess
As Steve turned round and said have I passed my test.

Trish Chandler

FORGOTTEN RING

The jumble sale was as it seemed,
Just bric-a-brac and bits of dreams,
Odd bits of glass and trinkets and things,
But there was one, odd coloured ring.

It fell from inside an old case
And threw out beauty, with such haste.
The colours shone, even in the dark,
Fluorescent, yet with uncanny spark.

Just what was the story of this jewel,
It shone like a rainbow's brilliant fuel,
Ancient, and from long gone times,
The silver marked with strange design.

Call it strange, call it unreal,
Things have a habit, often to reveal.
Coincidence as it may seem,
The ring had power so unforeseen.

The case was given, for a good cause,
And jumble brings to light many flaws,
The ring was a gift, one nearly forgets,
Memories sometimes fade, as old age regrets.

But curious to see what she could find,
The frail old lady was beckoned or some kind,
Her ring reached out, with memories of past years,
She bought back her treasure, with joyful tears.

William Nichol

WOMAN OF THE HEATH

I remember the first time I saw you dear
You were walking your dog on the heath
You caught a breeze and sneezed out loud
And your dog ended up wearing your teeth

Oh, how your hair swayed in the breeze
It was the colour of rusty tin
It looked so very thick and dark
As it sprouted from your chin

I remember the first meal we shared dear
It was the first time you'd sampled a winkle
And though you didn't care much for the taste
It sure gave your eyes a bright twinkle

Oh, how we kissed that very night
How we held each other near
You sucked so hard upon my tongue
It emerged right through your ear

Oh, what an animal lover you were dear
Your passion knew no bounds
And how you surprised me that autumn night
When I caught you in bed with the hounds

I remember you as the girl I once knew
In my mind you're still walking that heath
And though that day has long since gone
At least you're now wearing your teeth.

L J Pearce

FATHER WILLIAM (FEMINIST VERSION)

You are old, Mrs Woman, my looking-glass says,
And your hair will quite shortly be white,
Yet you walked through the town in Victorian dress -
Do you think at your age it was right?

In my youth, I replied, I was proper and prim
And never made anyone stare;
But now I'm prepared to dress up at the whim
Of our Hon Sec, my friend over there.

You are old, Mrs Woman, your face is all lined,
Said that looking-glass rudely to me;
Yet you rode on that tram - were you out of your mind
To exhibit yourself on TV?

A Victorian bonnet's as good as a screen
To hide wrinkles and multiple chins,
And many a varicose leg lurks unseen
'Neath the shelter of these crinolines.

You are old, said the glass, and you should have more sense
Than to play such undignified pranks.
The state's pensioned you off, at enormous expense,
So sit quiet and offer up thanks.

You have told me off thrice, and that is enough,
I informed the said glass on the wall.
Keep your thoughts to yourself, or I shall get tough
And just bin you - reflections and all.

Irene Howlett

MY NEW LIFE

When my husband died
As if I lost all my pride
It took me two years and over to finally discover
I am alone but not forever

Then one day I started thinking
That this is only a temporary dislinking
There were better things waiting for me
This new life I am living
I am happier than before
I only think for today
Tomorrow is a new day

I am a changed person
My life is not the same
The things I used to do before
I pushed them through the door
I can now sing and feel free
Now that my life is new
There is no more darkness in my heart
No more fears
Thank God that he listens to me
For my life is a life of prayers
I will not return to the olden days and ways.

Thelma Daniels

WITH ATTITUDE

The crabbed old man
bears a cardboard sign
reading *please talk to me*.
Those who have tried
studiously
cross the road,
whistling insultingly.

At Gatwick,
awaiting my flight,
there was another;
his T-shirt reading -
Leave me alone . . .
'Does it work?' I enquired,
and, baring his teeth,
he snarled -
'Usually'.

Ralf Bates

MY WONDERFUL PETS

When God almighty created animals
He filled my life with joy
A papolin dog Charlie Kismo
Such a loyal friend to me.
I've two budgies, colours, one
Green, one blue
They tweet and sing and
Alpha says I love Jesus too.
Then there's Tim my hamster
A lovely honey-coloured and white
He peeks out at me with his
Bright red eyes
Then I've two gerbils I called
Peter and Petra
They now have additions
Three baby gerbils.
They are so bold and make me laugh
As they scamper and play around.
They are all so cute
I simply thank God, for these wonderful pets
That brighten my life each day.

Maureen J Archbold

SMOKING HAZARDS

One day, when salting fish and chips,
a careless fag fell from my lips.
Smoked fish I'd had before, but ee!
Smoked chips were something new to me.

One day, when rendering a note
a careless fag slid down my throat.
The scream of pain filled me with glee:
I'd never struck so high a key.

One day, when bathing in my tub,
a careless fag fell on the scrub.
It flared right up! Oh well, oh my!
Who wants to scrub one's back? Not I!

One day, in bed, when lying in,
a careless fag rolled on my chin.
I shot up yelling: 'Damn and dash!'
I've now to sleep on blackened ash.

One day, when driving down a street,
a careless fag dropped on the seat.
I picked it up before it burned -
by then my car had overturned.

One day, when going for a roam,
a careless fag remained at home,
and, on returning down my road,
I found I had no fixed abode.

Just now, at service station rank,
a fag's dropped in my petrol . . .

Tony Hughes-Southwart

UNTITLED

Up the ale house
We laugh like Vikings,
Slap our thighs
And think up new things:

Like a fish out of water . . .
As thirsty as a fish . . .

At the party,
Where forgot is forgotten,
We manage to mould
A new eccentric for the morrow.

Like a fish out of water
and into the fire . . .

Lee Martin

A STICKY END

I found this stick insect,
one day on a walk,
so I took it back home,
and learnt it to talk.
I taught it some vowels,
consonants next,
read it some Shakespeare,
and Latin text.
He soon found words easy,
a genius was he,
he was invited to Windsor,
by the Queen to have tea.
But he ruined it all,
by bowing too far,
Prince Philip drove past,
and run him over in his car.

Rachel Oxtoby

LAUGHTER

Laughter is good for the soul they say.
Well I really out to know,
Because some days I laugh nearly all of the day.
After all, if you're sad, don't let it show.

Each day we face things that go wrong.
But does it really matter,
For if we react with a laugh and a song,
The sorrow we feel will soon scatter.

Life is for living, and live it we must.
So it's best to be happy and gay.
It's much better to laugh, and to laugh till we bust,
Than be sad, and to cry every day.

If we have a problem, and face it with calm.
Make it a challenge instead.
Then there will be no need for alarm,
Or a worry that we have to dread.

Look at life, and laugh at it,
For there is always some good to find.
It's like a jigsaw, and each piece will fit.
Perhaps laughter is all in the mind.

Jill Pettitt

THAT'S BUZZINESS

Said the bee unto the rose,
'A pollen uplift, I suppose?'
The rose replied, 'Quite right!
To yonder cutie, attired white,'
The bee now - 'Let me see,
I'll just work out the fee,
The lads and I agree,
With a free market economy.'

No rose or bee would shift,
To enable an uplift,
Intransigence o'er money,
Meant there was no bread and honey.

Thomas A Rattray

MECHANISTIC INEPTITUDES

When I climb into my car,
Turn the key and it doesn't start,
I get a flush beneath my collar,
Feel a shiver down my spine
And a palpitation of the heart.

And on my personal stereo,
When I try to select
A particular favourite track,
I press the button; fast forward,
But the tape winds back.

And in the early morning
In my bright pink bathroom
When I'm in a tearing rush,
I always seem unable
To get the lavatory to flush.

And when I tried to type
This poem on my computer,
I pressed 'Y' for 'save and replace',
But when I looked at the screen again
. . . It'd disappeared without a trace.

John Merritt

NEWSFLASH!

We interrupt this broadcast to report
Disturbing scenes to stop the live export
Of yoghurts meant for Continental markets
Where then they're packed in overcrowded baskets
Customarily they are then eaten
Live and sometimes they are even beaten
Protesters say this practice is barbaric
To which government response has been erratic.
Police tried to hold protesters back
Who, armed with missiles, started to attack
Lorries as they drove through the gates
Delivering the yoghurts in their crates.
Ugly scenes and insults then ensued
As attempts were made to have the crates rescued
By climbing over barriers and fences,
Police then stepped up their defences.
One woman to us tearfully described
Witnessed scenes of tortured yoghurts jibed
Whilst desperately running from the spoon
As discarded cartons on the ground were strewn.
Unverified reports are coming through
Of casualties, extensive damage too
Amidst the banners and the angry shouts
From protesters as the crowd openly flouts
The law in their resolve for humane treatment
Of yoghurts and to this demand agreement.
The slogan chanted to each lorry driven
Is 'Set them free from their plastic prison'.
We'll update you later on the situation
Meanwhile we return you to the cartoon animation.

Kim Montia

WOULD-BE POACHER

Well you can laugh,
But I'm telling you,
Ole Albert's bum,
Is black and blue.

He would go poaching,
I told him not to,
But he wouldn't listen,
So what can you do.

He took aim,
He got the pheasant,
He copped something else too,
That wasn't so pleasant.

A barrel full of buckshot,
Right up his backside,
I was laughing so much,
That I almost cried.

He hollered, he cussed,
The air was quite blue,
He hopped around shouting,
Who needs friends like you.

We got him home with a struggle,
We laid him on the kitchen table,
Get the medicine chest quick,
I called out to Mable.

All ended well though,
Poaching is not all honey,
I saw Albert yesterday,
And he ain't half walking funny.

Lindsey Jenkins

CHOCOLATE LOVE

We married on St Valentine's Day
In nineteen-sixty-four.
On such a day of romance
We couldn't wish for more.
The day was done, we had just a pound,
We thought we were in clover,
So Ian bought me a Mars Bar
With which to win me over.
Now every year on that day
With no substitute, or excuses,
A reminder of our undying love,
A Mars Bar he produces.
The trouble is, I meant to say
Some thirty years ago,
That Mars Bars were not to my taste:
I should have let him know!
But romance being what it is
I'm so afraid to say -
'Could you buy me something else?
Perhaps a Milky Way'.

Keren H Robertson

THE WORM

The garden worm is a creature
That is very underrated
He gets trodden on, chopped in half,
And with a rake, gets grated

Children pull him clean in half
Or throw him to the birds
He cannot fight, or even bite
He's a creature of very few words

If he's in the way of the lawnmower
It squashes him to a pulp
Or if a blackbird spies him
He swallows him in one gulp

So next time that you see a worm
Please don't treat him badly
And he will repay you very well
By turning your earth over, gladly.

Carol A Maddison

ANGLER'S DAY OUT

As I sit here, wrapped in my coat,
Watching this bloody orange float,
He goes off to relieve his bladder,
Leaves me here with his bag of . . .
. . . Sweetcorn smells and bum's gone cold,
'Just shut up will you,' I am told,
I've been sat here for bloody hours,
Under the brolly, in May showers,
I went to the toilet, there I found,
Loads of blood splattered all around,
I think it's gross, I'm quite appalled,
'A whinging woman,' I am called,
I think fishing's so frustrating,
I'm sick of all the bloody waiting,
Then with rod thrust in my hand,
I'm told by now, I should understand,
So then with shrieks of 'I can't do it,'
I am told 'Just bloody throw it,'
I know what fishing's all about,
For I've just thrown a perfect cast out!

Julie Thompson

SPIDER ON THE CEILING

When I go to bed at night
I always look to see
If a spider is in the ceiling,
Staring down at me.
There always seems to be one,
It's the same thing every night.
And he doesn't even move at all
When I switch on the light.
Every day he sits there,
In the same old place.
And I have to keep an eye on him,
Lest he vanish without a trace.
I don't know where he comes from,
Or who he comes to see.
I only know he is there each night,
And seems to look at me.
I'm told he will not harm me
And I'm sure it's true,
But I like to know if he's staying,
Or where he's going to.
I wonder if, when I'm asleep,
He'll crawl up and down the wall.
Or if he'll lose his grip
And onto my bed fall.
When I wake up in the morning
Before I go downstairs,
I look up at the ceiling,
Strange, the spider's never there.

Patricia Jamieson

THE TEA DANCE

We sat all three
Wallflowers we,
When up he came
Without a name,
So smart and dashing
We thought him smashing.
Who's it to be?
Why girls - it's me!
The oldest crock
In my best frock -
And so we danced
But not entranced.
He tut tut tutted
As I wrong-footed
And said to me
Quite nast-i-ly
Please concentrate upon the dance!
Upon his tone I took my stance.
How dare he talk this way to me
Who does he think that he can be
For I have paid my 50p!
For bickies and a cup of tea:
Meanwhile, the wallflowers thinking this
Is just sublime - the sheerest bliss,
Have got a shock in store for them
When Sheilah, the crème de la crème
Returns, her story to relate.
They just cannot believe her fate!
And laugh and laugh past every shoe shop
All down the high street to the bus stop!

Jill Barker

TIN HAT LOVES THE SLEEPY SNOWDROP

Chasing rainbows in the sky
Silk polka dot
Marshmallow pie
Dancing poppies
And paper torn
Chasing lightning
In the storm

Dancing angel in the sky
What seaweed green
To my surprise
Red golden green
The strangest fact
The holly land
The darkest black

Lazy daydreams in the sky
Hot knife burning
Passing by
The secret garden
And magic tea
Come break your mind
And set it free

Lee Robinson

MR BEAN

I am a little kidney bean
I want you all to know
My master plants me in the ground
So I will grow and grow

And when I get much bigger
I'm strapped against the wall
Because in his wisdom
My master knows it all

I'm feeling rather proud right now
I'm taller than the grass
And when I grow much taller
My beans will be amass

Don't think that I've had a bad life
For it is plain to see
I'm always going to be the best
With butter on for tea!

Frances Bennell

FOOD GLORIOUS FOOD

I really do love chicken and I like all kinds of meat,
But lots of things Mum gives me are impossible to eat.
Every day fresh vegetables, why did God make so many?
Broccoli, spinach, cauliflower and sprouts - I don't like any.
There are courgettes, aubergines, peas and beans, they really don't taste nice.
Why can't my Mum just give me plain chicken with my rice?
When I first get home from school I watch the children's hour
While my Mum cooks the dinner making sauce with milk and flour.
Oh heck! What's going in it - not leeks or broad beans, no!
I'm sure they must be poisonous and besides I hate them so.
Dinner's ready, Mum has called and I can't bear to see
Those horrid things upon my plate, they can't be good for me.
'If you eat all your veg,' Mum says, 'you can have your favourite pud;
It's chocolate sponge and custard and it really will taste good.'
But is my mother silly? It must be plain to see
That if I eat my dinner there'll be no room inside of me.
When I am a grown-up, left home and gone away,
I'll only eat jelly and ice cream for my dinner every day,
And crisps and cakes and chocolates, they are tastier by far,
And I think that they are good for me, in fact, I'm sure they are.

Susie Mehmed

SUMMER HOLIDAY

My landlady's Martha
Her husband is Arthur
I spend each day by the sea
The ice cream's inviting
The pier is enticing
With buttered scones served up for tea

I went to see Sadie
Billed as the fat lady
Who clearly lived life to the full
I sent Mum a postcard
The verse by a coarse bard
About a saucy young lass by a pool

The sun shines brightly
I dance almost nightly
The lager glides down like a treat
And daily I play
The amusement arcade
Or gaze at the sea from a seat

When I freeze in December
I'll still remember
This fortnight of ease by the sea
As I trudge down the street
Bombarded by sleet
I'll still feel the sun shines on me

Stuart Delvin

THE HOOKER'S LAMENT

Bury me in a Y-shaped coffin
That's where I want to be
Wearing scarlet lipstick, bright red rouge
And a skirt above my knee.

Bury me amongst the menfolk
Where I'll lay comfortably
They've been my bread and butter
But not always my cup of tea!

Bury me looking skywards
Whether overcast or sunny.
Did I do it for my country?
Yes, but also for the money.

Bury me in my home town
In my stockings and high boots.
Make sure I look my prettiest
And please touch up my roots.

Bury me with a headstone marked
'She's *really* now in heaven'
No need to show my date of birth
I stopped at thirty seven.

I'm buried in a Y-shaped coffin
So someone heard my plea
I died of natural causes
Doing what comes naturally.

J Susan Collins

I KNEW YOU COULD!

Proud I'm so proud,
I knew that you could,
Loud let's shout loud,
You said that you would.
You've given up smoking,
(Not a minute too soon!)
My prayers have been answered,
Yes! I'm over the moon.
So, Sis, keep it going,
Get them out of your life,
I know you'll get stronger and stronger.
They're costing you money,
also giving you strife,
Without them, you'll live so much longer!
I need you around,
On those days I feel down,
With your smile,
and that good listening ear.
So don't make me sad, or I might just get mad.
Then you know what,
might happen, I fear

I may have to start smoking!

Pauline Jones

THE DRESS

Party time all preparation,
My new dress is a sensation!
No one will have one like mine
I'll coyly stand and sip my wine
Enjoying the admiring glances
Expected in such circumstances.

But wait! What's that? And who is she?
Someone here dressed like me!
Not only did she 'twin my winner'
Her hair is blonder and she's thinner.

J Facchini

SQUASH AT FIFTY

With bald patch, flabby waist and spreading rear
but sharply dressed in all the proper gear:
flash pumps, trim shorts, smart shirt, sweat-bands - the lot,
I boast the ball (of course, the yellow spot)
and always 'play the game', a 'real good sport',
and try to smash opponents off the court.
Squash is like sex, always in fashion,
and when the adrenalin flows so does the passion
until the calming shower and drinks ice-cool.
I wonder why my wife thinks me a fool,
always expecting that fateful phone call
that I've collapsed in a heap - having slipped on the ball.
'I knew you would!' I clearly hear her say;
perhaps she's right - this dog has had his day!
Already I parade some vivid scars
adorning eyebrows, lips - trophies of war -
torn ligament, sprained wrist, blue-black toenail,
two pairs of shattered specs - a sorry tale.
So you can understand and sympathise
And see why now I play with just two eyes
squinting at wavering lines, fighting the years,
pathetically spraying sweat, blood, tears
on hard wood floor and even harder wall.
Then staggering home - triumphant, ten feet tall!

Ray Wilson

DAFT

I don't believe
What you just said
I think you are going
Right off your head

After all
What is it about
All you do
Is just scream and shout

Jumping up and down
All over the place
Chasing shadows
With increasing haste

I can't believe
That it was meant
And even more
How it was sent

Please tell me now
That it's all a dream
And that I haven't
Seen where I've been

Let me think
It's not all bad
And that may be
I've just been had

And when I wake
And have a laugh
It was all really
Just plain daft

Martin Booth

BURSTING THE BUBBLE

It first began, just to fill in time,
When both were at their physical prime.
But they never considered the aftermath
Of that night of passion, in the sunken bath.
My first memory, is of being trapped inside
A big, dark chamber that was very wide
There was no light, just a lot of flesh,
And regurgitated food, that was not very fresh.
As I grow, I begin to form,
And I start to like, the sac that's warm.
Now I have eyes and legs and arms,
As well as ears, to hear the bedside alarms
I'm getting too big, to be in this bubble,
If she doesn't get me out quick, there's going to be trouble
But it's me who's in strife, because it's only half-way,
At least that's what I hear, the doctor say
As time slumbers on, I begin to feel numb,
And I get hungry, so I chew on my thumb
I feel like a star, as I go for a scan,
It's a photo of me, to go with the clan
I need some rest, daytime I dread,
Because people keep patting my unseen head
I hear them say, would you like a girl or boy,
They speak of me, like I'm a returnable toy.
I've had enough now, after forty long weeks,
I'll make a break for that tunnel, from where the light peeks.
But she's taken some drug, that makes me go dizzy,
I don't need gas and air, I'm going to be busy
Here I am Mum, it's good to be free!
I'm glad that I'm out, because I want a pee.

John McIlhoney

THE FLYING FELINE

Harriet was abandoned, unloved and very small,
With tail as long and thin as she was thin and tall,
'Unlucky' was the name they gave her, whiskerless, one
ear bent o'er her,
Along came the soft-hearted Wilma, to whom Harriet did crawl.

The family nursed and loved this tiny grey-like ball,
Though she made poor Wilma trip and fall down in the hall,
They fed her vitamins and milk, she grew and grew, n'er
seen her ilk,
'Til they forgot she'd ever been a pathetic, scraggy scrawl.

Now husband was a golfer and keen on practise ways,
He putted in the garden and the house on dull, wet days.
One blustery Monday afternoon, he raised his club within
the room,
But didn't see poor Harriet sleeping on the chaise.

Positioning ball on carpet, husband gave the club a swing,
How good it felt, he must go now and give old George a ring
To tell him he could place a ball, by putting straight on
down the hall,
Till he saw dear Harriet a-flying on the wing!

The children saw the dreadful act, and wailing, crying all
Poor Dad felt sick inside, the cat stuck to the wall,
They picked her up, but she leapt down, and cowered, what
a frown!
They found her with broken leg, but unscathed overall.

Wilma came home as chaos reigned, and she was screaming too,
The vet came by, put Harriet in basket in the loo
Where it was warm and she slept sound, and children
whispered all around
But no one spoke to Dad who trembled in his shoe!

The 'free' cat story is a tale of warning to us all
Don't practise golf within the house, or e'en within the hall,
Vet's bills, one fifty quid adds up, it's cheaper if you
buy a pup,
So keep the cat away and safe when Dad's going to play a ball.

Elizabeth M Sudder

MR VIRTUAL REALITY

Enter . . .

The instructions declared user friendly,
Stated, that down loading was a breeze,
But it appears that Mr Virtual Reality,
Isn't all as compatible as seems,
His thirty-six bit memory,
Tends to crash from time to time,
And his puzzled look, leads me to believe,
That from the start he was never on line.
I've tried to interface with him,
But all I seem to get,
Is not at home, gone to lunch,
Or I'm out surfing the internet,
Maybe it's his micro-processors,
Or a simple problem with his main frame,
But no matter how good his graphics look,
I'm tired of playing his game,
Oh Mr Virtual Reality,
I think it's time to end,
This program of self-admiration,
So I'm pulling the plug, my virtual friend,

. . . Delete.

Skye Taylor

A GIRL NAMED FRED

A girl was born to the family 'Bear'.
She was born bald but she had some hair.
The tresses which ran down her back were red
'Tis a pity they were not on her head!

A beautiful girl she was christened Fred
And the warts on her face turned many a head.
Her clothes were made by a couturier
So everyone used to call her 'threadbare'.

Fred was a tall girl of three feet eight,
Kept appointments on time, always being late.
With her friend she ran races indoors all alone
And wore out the carpets, of which, she had none.

When the snow was raining it was odds on
She'd run barefoot with just her clogs on.
She was a tuneful singer but had no voice
And was forced to work hard, of her own choice.

Fred married a man with no head for heights -
A steeplejack - who stood up for his rights.
Of wooden legs he had but two
And Fred loved him dearly when the divorce came through.

As a keen athletic type she favoured field events
And when she picked the javelin up excitement was intense.
As well as opening the event, she very nearly shut it
And she would have put the shot that day but forgot where she had put it!

Finally, she retired, inland, on the coast.
She had no children and, of them, she would boast.
Fred died of old age at the age of twenty-four
And the rest of her life was simply a bore!

John W Skepper

PIGEON GOSSIP

Everyone knew each other's business,
In the street where I grew up,
I remember it like it was yesterday,
When I was just a young pup.

We kids played out in the street,
From morning till very late,
So we knew what was going on,
For instance,
In the house with door number eight.

One by one the windows would close,
To keep in the terrible din,
But tempers would raise to fever pitch,
So we'd hear what went on within.

Then a race began amongst us kids,
To see who could spill the beans fast,
To our mothers we would scurry,
And stretch a tale that would last and last and last.

If we thought a reward was at hand,
For that juicy bit of scandal,
We thought wrong I would say,
As our ears felt the end of a sandal.

Before the sting had left our ears,
The gossip had been carried,
As if on the wings of a pigeon,
To a couple who recently married.

Ruth Hughes

MUSICAL SAM

An eccentric avant-garde musician,
whose stage name was 'Musical Sam'.
Severed one arm with his musical saw,
and it fell to the floor with a bang.
Undaunted, he changed his repertoire
and his fame spread right through the land,
now he tours the country, billing himself,
as 'Sam and His Single Hand Stand'.

Michael Griffith

EVEN JESUS HAD A WARM-UP MAN

You never know how good they are
When they're support act for the star
Applause is rarely very loud
As they rise upward through the crowd.

Warm-up bands I've dismissed with groans
Include the Animals and Rolling Stones
Others I've ignored in bars,
Turn up one day as superstars

Comics weird and really witty
get booed off stage and, more's the pity,
We don't look fondly at these blokes
'Til they're on the telly telling jokes

Carrying anger that's backdated
From times they weren't appreciated
And it's pretty galling to discover
That I was just your warm-up lover.

Mike Hoy

THE GENUINE ARTICLE

Copper jug
dented by years of use
now sits by the fireplace
displaying its sweet rusty shine
and distorting a twisted face

What age
did it first meet its lid
that looks over a solid body
Despite its densely dusty skin
it is proud of this parody

On a table
a wimpled woman pours
her haste her simple perfection
not wanting to keep madam waiting
the jug shows no connection

Roman house
an orgy is in full flow
a eunuch pours the drinks
out to hot whores and centurions
but no one even blinks

Even Jesus
may have used this vessel
to produce the abundant wine
but this is very very unlikely
as it was made in 1989
never mind

Andy McPheat

OH SOCKS!

Twenty two lonesomes lying in a row
Oh where! Oh where! Does the other one go?
Mixed in with washing of bulky load
Why don't they come out again does anyone know?
A full load, a half load, the result is the same
So is hide and seek an ankle socks game?
I thought I could foil them if that was their plan,
But another one later, outwitted I am.
Stuff them in stockings, I thought, must be the way,
Then pair them up carefully, but you'll still hear me say,
I've got another one, here all on its own,
I just can't believe how the odd pile has grown.
I check the washed garments, the jumpers and frocks,
In case one is lurking . . . a renegade sock.
Zip them in a bag I thought, that should surely catch em,
But later down hearted I just could not match them.
So where is its partner did it dive down the drum?
Gobbled and spit out as fluff sounds no fun.
Impossible notion, mechanic he says,
But shakes his head baffled as I show him one less.
Now twenty four lonesomes lying in a row,
Oh where? Oh where? Does the other one go?

Jane Darnell

PARENTAL PROBLEMS

Kids pose their parents awkward questions,
Why, when, what, where, who?
And when it comes to giving answers
the onus falls on you

There are some age old questions
'bout babies, love and sex,
these are the ones you fear the most
and make you feel perplexed

As your offspring learn and grow
the queries are more puzzling
'Why is the earth round, not flat,
and where on earth is Nuzzling?'

But I am left wanting to know
when parents ask their offspring,
these same kids gaze up vacantly
'Whad'd'ya mean, *washing*?'

Angela Smith

DECKCHAIR BLUES

The funniest thing that springs to mind,
Trying to set it up at the time,
Is watching my husband with a deckchair,
Moving it every way, it landed in the air.

We couldn't keep our faces straight,
The tears were rolling down at such a rate,
Suddenly we had to look away,
He turned to us in such dismay.

After a while he got it right
And sat down with such delight,
The best laugh was yet to come
As he went right through it, landing on his bum.

Every time I think of that scene,
Tears of laughter begin to stream,
Whenever I tell this funny tale,
You can be sure it never will fail.

Evelyn M Harding

THE FATE OF A FLEA

The funniest thing that I ever did see
Was watching a monkey catch a flea
It swung by one arm with the other was scratching
There must have been a lot of them hatching
He scratched from his head to the tip of his toes
Then right back up the inside of his nose
Jumped down from the branch to be with his mum
Had another quick scratch caught the flea on his bum
The poor little flea met a terrible fate
Monkey was hungry so poor flea got ate

Angela Pearson

THE VICAR'S VISIT (TRUE)

My friend and I were having tea
when I saw the vicar coming along, to visit me
I quite forgot he was coming to see me,
I jumped up quickly and into my lap, went my cup of tea
it was hot, so very hot, oh dear me!
I dashed to the kitchen . . . and tore off my knickers
mopped at my dress
then grabbed an apron to cover the mess
There was a knock at the door,
no time to do anything more
I opened it with a smile . . .
the vicar stayed quite a while!
I caught my friend's eye
and tried not to giggle
as I felt very damp and wanted to wriggle
We couldn't share the joke, with the vicar . . .
for how was he to know
it didn't show
that I was without knickers!

Edna Parrington

SONNET FOR A WEDDING

We are not bound together by the law
Nor by gold rings or vows that we have made
But by the hopefulness of our two hearts
That see into the future unafraid.
Today we join the choir where families sing
As tunefully as any nightingale
When on a summer's evening from dark trees
A song pours out whose beauty cannot stale.
It tells of peaceful times that are to come
As in bad weather we are armed for pain
By sheltering love, so that we surely need
No laws to keep us from the driving rain.
Our names are written in the book of life,
A faithful husband and a loving wife.

Deirdre Armes Smith

SHAPE UP

Can't help it if I'm a strange shape
It's the way that life has made me.
Chin up, chest out, tummy tucked in
Shoulders back, think tall and slim.
That's what they said at school - in army -
Heaven help us, are they barmy?
Keep your head up do not droop
Don't want to end up with a stoop.
Then they said keep chin tucked *in*,
In or up? - poor confused chin.
So I grew another one
And let them choose
It's much more fun!

Kathleen Jarrold

MAN'S BEST FRIEND

Oh pussy said the doggy
You may put your trust in me
For I really am a softie
I'm not interested in thee.

Just look into my big brown eyes
I really would not hurt a fly
I do not care how much they buzz
They are just not worth the fuss.

I've had my meat and biscuit dinner
I may even get a snack for supper
So jump down off the fence cat do
I'll walk along the lawn with you.

Fooled you cat, you are so dumb
I do enjoy a bracing run
Hey, come on cat no need to spit
I only want to play a bit.

Put those claws away dear chap
There's no need to act like that
If I back off, you can run away
But I'll get you another day.

Bernard Grose

THE LEG MAN?

I am a handsome table leg.
I stand straight and tall.

Being a rectangular structure,
there are four of us in all.

We loyally support the table,
through good times and lean.

So how come it's always getting laid,
whilst we have never been?

Pauline Brennan

KISS ME QUICK

Christmas is over and next year's goose is getting fat
Holiday adverts are on the telly, Christmas bills are on the mat
Saving for a week away to get away from it all
Sun, sea, sexual piracy time to have a ball
The holiday is nearly here time to pack your case and bags
Waiting in anticipation the next few days start to drag
Now it is time to travel, planning and scheming ahead
Kiss me quick in a night-club, another conquest in bed
The hotel room is like a cell, time to head for the beach
Mad dogs in the midday sun, skin burnt, hair bleached
Before too long it's night time and a club is the next stop
The alcohol takes control time to boogie 'til you drop
You spy someone you fancy amongst the heaving throng
No need for inhibitions, you know it won't be long
You smooch and writhe to Marvin Gaye holding each other tight
Sexual healing becomes sexual feeling an urge too strong to fight
The bedroom is more private and you do what you have to do
Out of a sense of duty lust takes hold of you
Now it is all just memories and you have never felt so pleased
Just a suntan to remind you and a *sexually transmitted disease.*

Dave Lunn

OUT FOR FUN

Watch the youngsters as they play
They're like this almost every day.
First running this way and then the other
At times controlled by their loving mother.

At times a fight of the mocking kind,
Into as much mischief as they can find.
Full of life, and they don't give a damn,
See how they fight over a piece of ham.

The chase is on to see who is best,
Round and round the room, a real test.
Now into the garden for a special treat;
Till mum rounds them up, now there's defeat.

They did no harm, it was just a sham,
Then someone shouts, 'Now there's that ham'.
I wonder if it's time to now own up.
Well what do you expect from a little pup.

Mike Lowe

MY LOVE, MY LADA

I love my little Lada, all shiny bright, and new
I drove it down the motorway, and it reached fifty-two

So every Sunday morning, no matter rain or shine
I get my sponge and bucket out, and clean off all its grime

But as I washed the windscreen, and much to my dismay
I went and broke a wiper off - that really spoilt my day

I pulled my hat and coat on, and put away my mop
I drove it to a garage, and rushed into the shop

'I'd like some windscreen wipers, for my Lada, sir' I said
And pointed out the window, to my car, all shiny red

He scratched his head and pondered, and looked at me real strange
Then smiled, and said 'OK ma'am, that seems a fair exchange!'

Sally Storer

FOUR LETTERS

OK who's the wise guy or gal,
Certainly nobody's pal,
Whoever invented that four letter word,
Such a vast response, it's absurd.

Thousands of people all over the planet,
Some people have even managed to can it,
Others make millions and millions of dosh,
It's everyone's problem, the poor to the posh.

Would the world be a larger and happier place
If this little word was lost without trace,
Hundreds of methods that people will try,
All could have power to make a man cry.

I know I've tried them, every which way,
But it always comes back, it just seems to stay,
Forget all the boiling, you might as well fry it,
Someone see sense and ban the word *diet!*

Amanda Giddings

A DAY IN THE LIFE OF YOURS TRULY

They say laughter is the best tonic,
Probably after wishing someone 'Good Health',
I can't guarantee a laugh in this
But it's left me gasping for breath.

It's half past eight, I've woke up late
As off to the bathroom I toddle,
Get washed and dressed apply war-paint
For the day ahead to tackle.

I've fed my hubby, walked the dog
Dusted around, made the bed
Blow in my 'Peak Flow' the pointers down
Then mark on the graph what I have read.

The next trip is on my bike,
Where's the ruddy list I mutter,
The 'road hogs' go flying by
A few choice words I utter.

The shops are busy, I meet a friend
Who's poetry like-minded too,
As we discuss poetry over the veg
Just remembered the rolls for the loo.

I'm homeward bound to make the lunch
Then do some gardening maybe walk the dog,
My hubby calls 'He wants some fish,
That dog thinks he's a mog'.

Times flown by, It's dinner time,
As my poor heart gives a heave
That pile of ironing won't disappear
No use to moan or grieve.

Evening time is my time,
I have no wish to roam
What is it that poets do best?
Just write another poem.

Joyce White

BELLOWS

The bellows lying next to me is my old man
Snoring loud as only the male nostrils can
The trumpeting proboscis on his face is a disgrace
The honking hooting thing wants shooting.

I lie with quiet breath and listen to the rumble
Trying to ignore each momentary mumble
The waffling, whiffling rasps are all a jumble
Mine is, of course, a mere respiratory ripple.

His breathing in is not so bad as is his breathing out
Somehow I stop myself from smothering the offending snout
He seems to blast out more than ever he gasped in
The huff and puff and all that stuff make such a din.

But worst of all to bear, of course, is this -
The self-indulgent smacking of his lips
As though he so enjoys his sonorous and slumberous state
While I am left to count the withering hours as they abate.

If I should utter even one word of complaint
He is affronted as a dumb and blameless saint
'I never snore or snort more than I ought
But if you should have e'er cause to complain
Well then, I never will do it again'
And drops he instantly without repent
Into the deep snore of the innocent.

Roberta Reilly

THE HALL OF MIRRORS

I'm tall and slim, and very neat.
Is that me, I look a treat.
Then I move on, and look so fat,
Or is that me, do I look like that.
What have we next, I've shrunk to the floor.
I look about four foot four.
Which shall I be, six foot three.
I'm really confused, which is me.
Back to the true mirror, and out through the door,
I'll stay as I am, I won't complain any more.

Janet Isherwood

ILLUMINATION

(for Jenny and Peter)

Twinkle, twinkle harbour lights
Marking unbecoming sights
That some count as wicked but
Might be worse with a power-cut.

Twinkle, lights of old St Mawes,
Twinkle on without a pause;
Winking lewdly through the night;
I'll not respond - I'm too polite.

Twinkle, twinkle, Cornish lights
Advertising Cornish sites;
Cornish speech; the piskie theme;
Pasties, fish and clotted cream.

Jim Finch

ODES TO THE FAIR WEATHER ROWER

O to be a fair weather rower,
To go out when the sky is always blue,
And there's no wind chill factor,
To turn my skin blue.

O to be a fair weather rower,
To be always dressed in Lycra.
I have no fashion sense,
And the colour couldn't be any brighter.

Peter Altoft

POOR GROOM

As he walked up the aisle,
With his simple-like smile,
He waited to meet his poor doom.
The man thought to himself,
'That's the end of me wealth,
'Cause as it turns out, I'm the groom'.

The gullible bride,
Just stood by his side,
She had waited for this lovely marriage.
The groom summed up her weight and thought,
What a state.
'I reckon we needed a carriage!'

The bride dressed in white,
Was more clothed with fright,
But that was expected, of course.
With his price tag behind,
Something dwelt in his mind,
'When on earth can I get a divorce?'

Mandy Tatum

CALLED TO ACCOUNT

Can you ring Silvester dear,
The one with funny shoes,
You know - he has a mobile phone,
And always bills and coos.

Can you ring Virginia son,
She seems to have the blues,
You know - the one that talks for hours,
And always bills and coos.

Sons and daughters on the phone,
The tears, the fears, the thrills,
The 'coos' are fine, what I don't like
Are all those b . . . 'bills'!

Dave Priest

CONFUSING, ISN'T IT?

When you drive a car in France,
You must drive on the right;
As, over there, right is correct -
Remember that; all right?

When Frenchmen drive cars over here,
This rule is much abused;
Since, over here, the left is right -
No wonder they're confused.

Yes, left is right; and if,
Of common sense, they've got a speck,
They'll know that right's not left, but wrong.
Now I'm confused. Oh, heck!

Roger Williams

A SCHOOL OF LUNCH BOXES

Oh why am I so well endowed there has to be a reason
Perhaps the midwife stumbled and had nothing else to seize on
Well out of proportion but that's surely not my fault
Possession of a deadly weapon and liable to assault.
The other schoolboys thought me strange and really somewhat odd
But I was still quite happy at being called 'tripod'
'Cause when I took my Y-fronts off there came a deafening thump
'Stick it in your ear' they cried, 'you are a petrol pump!'
It wasn't until later that I came to realise
That I was blessed with what it took including length and size
For when I walked across the street the girls they all would whistle
Their sparkling eyes and looks of awe with thoughts of throbbing gristle.
Standing tall before me she had her see through dress on
Stay behind at school today you have an extra lesson
It didn't take me very long to consider what she taught us
A sudden stirring in my loins that turned to rigor mortis.
She moaned and groaned and screamed and shouted
Well before I'd even mounted
Standing to attention and ready for the action
But two weeks later I was in remorse for she was still in traction.
It hasn't really put me off but now I'm rather placid
Laying naked in my bed you couldn't call it flaccid
Hold on tight 'cause here I come I shout with satisfaction
Another newsflash, another earthquake sweeps across the nation.

So don't forget the next time you're laying in your bed
Try to convince your partner it's safer to give head.

G Holland

THE DREAM

Two old bowlers were sat chatting
on an old park bench seat,
by the side of the club bowling green,
where they would often meet.
'Last night I had the strangest dream'
the first one said.
'With my bowls bag in my hand I was on
my way to heaven, I dreamt that I was dead!'

'St Peter took me by the hand when
I arrived at the pearly gate.
Saying tomorrow is our annual bowls
match, I'm glad that you're not late.
This will be one bowls match you will
be glad you haven't missed.
I am going to make you captain, because
you are top of my bowlers list!'

The second bowler laughed as he said,
'I bet you are glad it was only a dream?'
Back came the reply, 'So should you be,
you were down as captain of the opposing team!'

D Norman

POETS ARE . . .

Poets are a brazen crop,
Hiding passions barely.
Scribble, scribble 'til they drop
Wordbloomers every . . . wherely!

Poets are a scruffy breed
Of mongrels rough an' ready.
Walkies! Walkies! As they lead
Up garden paths wordheady!

Poets are a loony crowd
Who 'ink' they are quite normal?
Softly . . . softly . . . not so loud;
Brit poets? Mad but formal!

'Poets are a dying race.'
Who said that . . . are you mental?
Pooh, pooh, I'm living proof - in case
I'm wrong . . . my brain's on rental!

James Parry

CAKES FOR FUN

Making a cake with loving care
Just for my friends to share.
Fingers crossed it came out right,
So they'd enjoy the first bite!
When asked if there was more,
Well, I knew that cake would score!

It was someone else's turn to bake,
Now we've been promised chocolate cake!
Very delicious, so hard to beat,
Smothered in icing, what a treat!
We didn't have to ask for more,
For there was apple cake to score!

Now to turn this into some fun,
For this cake must be number one!
A brick covered in icing, just right,
Cutting it was a bit of a fight!
Afraid no-one asked for more,
But the laugh was the biggest score!

Penelope Ann

FLATULENCE

Have you ever been in a queue
and had a sudden urge to do
a big let off, whoops, sorry, pooh!
Everyone turns and looks at you
and you feel your face turn a reddish hue.
You walk away so harassed,
you've never felt so embarrassed,
you come back later to join the same queue
and hope that nobody recognises you.

Teresa Austin

HUBBLE, BUBBLE, DRINK AND TROUBLE

I've got this dear friend
Who to the bitter end
Is loyal and oh so kind
She makes me laugh
Drinks pints 'no, not halves'
A better friend I could never find.
She is perfectly able
To drink you under the table
Just try her, nothing will stop her,
Not even the rotter, who gets her blotto,
And gives her drinks in bottles, with wrong labels,
But please don't despair for,
She knows that, when I'm there
I'll join her and oh boy that means trouble
We don't really care
As when caught we'll declare
It wasn't us, it was the drinks in a muddle.

Carol Turner

DON'T YOU KNOW

Don't you know life's better when you're laughing
Don't you know it's sweeter when you smile.
Don't you know that life is just for playing
Making others happy all the while.

Don't you know it's better to be cheerful
Don't you know it's great to be alive.
No one wants to know you if you're tearful
Don't you know it's better to be blithe.

It's more exciting to be happy
To fill your life with tons of joy
Show your friends that you are jolly
Know you've 'been there', just like Kilroy

Don't you know life's better when you're friendly
Don't you know you're sweeter when you smile
Don't you know that life is there to play
Making others happy all the while -
Making others happy -
Making others happy -
Making others happy with your smile!

Nelson Peters

THE HONEY BEE

I wish I were a honey bee a-flyin' round the garden
Until I lands upon a stone and thinks 'cor that's a hard 'un
I flaps me wings and shakes me legs but I can't fly no more
Don't say I'll spend the rest of time a-stuck 'ere on this floor
I twists and turns and heaves and pulls but still me feet won't shift
I can't collect me pollen now - 'cor blimey I am miffed
I'll have to wait until it rains perhaps then I'll get free
If not - I'm very sorry folks - it's marmalade for tea.

Lyn Pratt

RELUCTANT FRIENDSHIP

I hold my voice, I bite my tongue,
There are things that can't be said.
Although you're meant to be my friend
I sometimes wish you dead.

I try my best to be polite,
To keep my feelings concealed,
But, sometimes I can't help myself,
They end up being revealed.

You say it once, you say it twice,
Then you say it three times more.
As though I can't hear you talking,
You really are a bore.

You're worse when you get really drunk
And fall down on your butt
You're really an embarrassment.
Sometimes you are a slut.

You think you're really interesting
And you think you're pretty cool.
Think you're the hardest girl around
But you are just a fool.

It's a shame you can't see your faults
Can't see what makes you so bad
I pity you, I really do
You really are quite sad.

These words I speak, you know they're true
And I speak them from the heart
My life is hell when you're around
But, great when we're apart.

Jennifer Emery

LIKES AND DISLIKES

Some people like peas pudding
Others like jellied eels
Some like savaloys and dips
Others like Wagon Wheels
Some people they like salads
Others like red meat
Some like ducks with veils on
Others like pigs' feet
Some like those big bull whelks
That chew like India rubber
Others like the taste of shrimps
While Eskimos like blubber
Some people they like oysters
It does their sex life good
Others prefer a pint of beer
As long as it's from the wood
Some people like black pudding
With great big lumps of fat
Some people they prefer a dog
While others like a cat
That's all I'm trying to tell you
No two people are the same
Each one is made to be different
They think life is just a game
I'll have this; you have that;
You'll often hear them cry
The only time they'll be the same
Is on the day they die
You think, that must be the finish
Oh no! 'Tis a sad tale I have to tell
While one went up to heaven
The other went down to hell
            That was the finish

Albert Gormley

BLUE SKIES, BLUE RINSE

Fat ladies in tights and fatter cars.
Over-stuffed over-burdened tin roof racks.
Suitcases bulging like creatures from Mars
Hungry for a visit to the doughnut shacks.

Old men who wear cardigans in spite of the sun,
Who talk about times when they splashed in the sea.
Now loafing on loungers remembering fun,
Forgetting how it was to be sand castle free.

Kids chomping on sand to their parents' dismay,
A munching a-crunching a-chewing away.
Blue skies, blue rinse, high life, high tide,
Oh I do hate to be beside the seaside.

Stout ladies with ankles as big as your head,
Red cheeks aflame with the sea wind's call.
Thin men walk behind like the last living dead,
In her shadow he walks, in her shadow he'll fall.

Burgers and onions are rammed up my nose,
From no recognisable part of a cow.
Stall holders screaming traditional prose,
'Roll up, spend too much money, right now!'

Parents swilling beer to their children's dismay.
Bored husbands watch bingo as sad housewives play.
Throwing up all over the carousel ride.
Oh I do hate to be beside the seaside.

Darren Stapleton

MY DONKEY

Have you seen my donkey? He escaped the other day
I really couldn't understand why he had to run away
The gentleman I bought him from said that his name was Kerby
And that with a bit of training he would win the donkey derby
I never will forget the day that animal arrived
Too large he was for to bring in, so he had to stay outside
For hours he stood like granite beside the coalshed wall
And no matter how I coaxed him, he wouldn't budge at all
So finally I decided this animal I would ride
I managed to struggle upon his back while he moved from side to side
But my head felt rather dizzy as he turned around and round
And then upon its bended knees, it fell upon the ground
I thought that I had killed the brute
For I knew I was overweight
Then he let out a wild harsh bray and gave me a look of hate
He finally struggled to his feet, I knew he would survive
Until I lost a lot of weight on him I wouldn't ride
I eat less at the table for I wanted to be slim
And I started doing exercises to keep myself in trim
A neighbour then suggested a method not known to fail
Give him a drop of alcohol, it would make him lift his tail
From a short time when he got it we heard an awful din,
And believe me he cleared the four foot fence and broke the rubbish bin
The method it did work all right for we haven't seen him since
It's the best cure for a donkey that wouldn't move an inch
He's likely around some public house either drinking gin or wine
So if you see him ring me up, my number's nine nine nine.

Marina Cardwell

THE CHOSEN WORD

Three friends in a group
chatting . . . smiling . . . spending
lottery millions on dreams
till one strode away.
Silent gaze . . . low whispers
follow in her stride,
I do declare
her weight she cannot hide . . .
A puffy face . . . *steroids!*

Over tea with a friend
the gossip was spread,
poor Bertha . . . now so fat . . .
Asteroids is that!
Can it be right?
Bertha in the sky at night . . .
A bright new star of the Milky Way
revolving in the universe
for ever and a day?

Clever are words
in whatever context
but nothing so complex
over gossip and tea . . .
When imagination flow
to Bertha's fate bestow.
Banished to spin in space
due to her puffy face . . .
A star-fish reflected in the sea.

Shirley Silman

WISHING

I get so hungry for food I can't wait
I'm trying to diet but just can't lose weight
I eat loads of chocolates, and thick steaks on a plate,
And that's why the lady is a frump.

I like to dance drink eat chips in a bag
I'll never be slim about that I can't brag
I eat crunchy biscuits tons of cream cakes
And that's why the lady is a frump.

Why? Don't I resist them give myself a break.

I look in the mirror my figure I hate
And that's why the lady is a frump
Is there a chance or is it my fate
Have I left it too late to lose weight.

Joan Bale

SLIMMER'S ENCOURAGEMENT

Gibraltar is a memory past,
Where 3 years slipped by very fast.
But I recall amusing one,
While sitting bathing in the sun,
Joined by locals for the day,
I overheard the granny say,
'I trying hard to lose some weight,'
As she tucked back tapas off her plate.
When all were happy and well fed,
A gust of wind took the hat from her head.
To which her daughter smiled with glee,
'Why Mama! You have lost weight see?'
'Your head is smaller, you doing well'
Convinced, was really, hard to tell.

Veronica Sharples

HELPFUL HINTS

In case of emergency don't pull the chain,
Sail in the gutter, slide down the drain.
Bounce a banana, try skipping with eels,
Swallow a lamppost . . . see how it feels.
Cuddle a cactus, juggle with jelly,
Hop round the block with blancmange in your welly.
Harpoon a slug. Comb your hair with a kipper.
Slurp Vintage Champagne from you grandad's old slipper.

In event of disaster go sit in a box.
Make nourishing sandwiches out of your socks.
Stuff a whole fruitcake right up your nose,
Suck tea through a hose-pipe . . . see how it flows.
Drink from a plate and eat from a cup . . .
What a terrible rhyme: who on earth made it up?
Brush your teeth with the dog, brush the floor with your brother,
And don't say this poem in front of your mother.

Dorothy Kershaw

HAPPY BIRTHDAY YOU'RE 60 NOW

You're 60 now it's plain to see,
By the varicose veins below your knee.
Teeth falling out, eyes growing dim.
Hair gone grey and getting thin.
You walk much slower and stoop a bit,
The clothes you once wore, now don't fit.
A zimmer frame I have placed on order,
Just to help you cross the border.
As you can see I love you dearly,
It's a shame you can't see me more clearly.

H Parker

BEFORE

I know I've walked this earth before, it's more than just a feeling.
I've sailed the seas and roamed the moors, and I haven't just been dreaming.

I've felt a sense of grandeur of living in a mansion.
I've ruled the roost and shouted orders at those beneath my station.

I've looked out of my windows at the acres that were mine.
I wonder how I came to be a lady dressed so fine.

I didn't want for anything, it was handed on a plate.
The jewels, the clothes, the luxuries, servants that hid their hate.

How did I come to be so rich, that's what puzzles me?
Did I commit some awful crime, and cause others misery?

I've wandered through my mansion with the feeling I belong.
There in all that splendour, how could it be so wrong?

It must have been an era when poverty was rife,
And I can't say in honesty, I had a better life.

There was a sense of loneliness and fear that I lived through,
Along with other tragedies and things I can't undo.

But I've always had this feeling that I have lived before.
Always been so well off, never, never poor.

So if I ever live again, I hope I find my mansion,
Instead of scraping through, on a measly old age pension.

I want to ride and roam the moors and do all the things wealth brings
I'm sick of making both ends meet, I'm designed for better things.

Dorothy Tinson

THE DRIVING TEST

When Alice took her driving test
She was a wee bit tense
But realised, that logically
Driving was common sense

She glanced at her examiner
Gave him a winning smile
He did not return the gesture
And thought the lass had guile.

He told her to drive forwards
Then take the next left turn
She ended up in someone's drive
The examiner looked stern

Her three point turn was almost four
The hill stop a disaster
She tried to do it in reverse
Which did not please the master.

Reversing wasn't her strong point
She hit the kerb instead
The emergency stop was even worse
The examiner bumped his head.

The test was almost over
And the questions came in last
She smiled at him so sweetly
Then whispered '*Have I passed?*'

Olive Cason

PRINCE CHARMING'S BALL

It was Prince Charming's birthday
And arriving at the hall,
Were all the cast of Pantoland
To hold the royal ball (!)
The Seven Dwarfs stood drinking
In a corner with Snow White,
But the wine was far too strong -
They held each other up all night!
Miss Muffet cried, 'I'm starving -
That old spider stole my lunch',
And as she reached the table -
Saw Tom Thumb fall in the punch!
'I see you've brought your beanstalk, Jack',
Smiled sheepishly Bo-Peep,
Young Sleeping Beauty stared so much -
She sent herself to sleep!
'Those sisters just get uglier!'
Laughed Buttons to Dick Whittington,
'They squeeze themselves into those gowns -
I don't know how they fit in 'em!'
Two elves stepped forward with a gift -
'Oh! Leather boots,' Prince cried,
'You must work in the shoemakers',
'Yes - cobblers!' they replied.
Then suddenly the clock struck twelve
And Cinders shrieked aloud,
And turning from a princess was -
'*A frog?!*' exclaimed the crowd.
'Oh well', sighed Prince, 'it makes a change -
It's usually *my* call -
At least she can't start nagging -
So I'm off to *have a ball!*'

Lynda Ann Green

STAGE STRUCK

Standing on a stage a laugh to win
Baring the soul is a mortal sin
A hostile audience there to be captivated
The comic has a chance of being decapitated

The room is full and the smoke is thick
The comic is going down like a big red brick
He has got to be careful where he is treading
He's going down like pork at a Jewish wedding!

The room is full and the smoke is thick
The audience are delivering a lot of stick
He presses on with a sullen sigh
Hoping against hope he will not die

'Get off the stage, you're a load of crap!'
Shouts a thick set navvy in a big black cap
'Say something funny!' yells a youth called Bunny
The comic begins to worry - will he get his money?

He then takes a breath and smiles
Feeling he is again on trial
'A few good gags and they'll be mine'
Said Johnnie Wager, in his mind

Zephyr Beau-Bradley and Robert Benton

MOMENT OF TRUTH

That's it, I've thrown in the towel,
Time has caught up with me at last,
Now I know I'm getting old,
My youth is in the past.

Whatever can it be, I hear you ask,
That makes me admit defeat?
- I couldn't see without my glasses
To pedicure my feet!

Margaret Burgess

THE FLU BUG

I think I've caught the flu bug
Because I don't feel very well
My poor head aches
And for goodness' sake
My eyes are starting to swell

My throat it feels so sore
My legs and arms are weak
I will go to my bed
Put a pillow on my head
And try to have a good sleep

I wonder how I caught it
I usually shrug things off
But because I feel low
The flu's got me I know
And now I'm starting to cough!

Perhaps I'll take some aspirin
Oh no, they're bad for the heart
A big glass of whiskey
Will make me feel frisky
So, I'd better take that for a start!

J Campbell

BEING 'PATIENT'

I tried to lift the patient but he would not leave his seat.
The sister yelled:
'You wally, you're standing on his feet!'
I said, 'I'm really sorry', and tried to make amends.

But as I stooped to get his slippers, I trod upon his lens.
'I truly am so sorry, I didn't see them there.'
'Is this your tie that's trapped beneath the chair?'
'Try to keep calm sir, I'll have it out in a sec!'

But as I bent to release the tie,
A finger caught him squarely in the neck!
'Please forgive me sir; you see, I'm fairly new around here.'

'Oh that's all right dear, I've had rough treatment before . . .
Now when was it . . . ? Ah I remember, it was as a prisoner of war!'

Neville Hawkins

LOVE OR MONEY

She was twenty seven
And I was ninety three,
But Jesus Christ that Woman
Had some kind of hold over me!

I was on the ebb tide
She skipped and danced everywhere she went
Her life was just beginning,
Whilst mine was almost spent!

Now I'm in my coffin
I can see my behaviour was rash,
I lie six feet underground
And she has all my cash!

Bob Darvell

THE DEAN, THE COCK AND THE HOUND

The dean had a fine coop of hens,
And one day he declared a wish,
To choose from his flock a fat black cock
To roast for his Sunday dish.

So he sent for a little choirboy
To catch and pluck the chicken bare,
And the busy boy plucked - wiff-waff, wiff-waff -
With the feathers flying everywhere.

Now the dean had a street-wise hound
Who watched the black feathers fly,
And when the little lad went to fetch the pan,
He ran off with the cock, on the sly.

Then the dean accused his pious monks
Of sinful gluttony and greed,
And examined each one to see if he grew plump
From having a good hearty feed.

But as each monk shrank in dismay
The hound it was who had the bloat,
And he started to swell and his muzzle went green
As they pointed to the culprit's throat.

Then the dean felt sorry for his plight,
And dosed him with camomile tea,
And so forgiven, the hound now sings
At matins with solemn piety.

Black feathers in the air,
Wiff-waff, wiff-waff, wiff-waff -
Black feathers flying everywhere.

Esme Francis

A NICE LEG OF PORK . . .

The stormy seas ten years before
had tossed young Jack upon the shore
along with Babe, the ship's pet pig
and Butch, his dog - mad, mean . . . and *big!*

Nine foodless days had made Jack thin
and thoughts to eat them had crept in
but he found Butch was *far* too smart
and Babe's sweet nature'd won his heart

So Jack had learned to fish and farm
and thus his pets came to no harm
In time, he loved the island life -
no boss to please, no nagging wife

But in his lonely hours of leisure
Jack's thoughts turned to carnal pleasure
He hit the bottle, but each swig
increased his passion for the pig

Now Butch liked not his master's kind
and when he grabbed Babe's vast behind
the dog did bark and growl at Jack
who backed off, fearful of attack

One dark-skied day, rough seas once more
threw deathly form upon the shore
Jack's kiss of life met warm soft mouth
inciting stirrings deep down south . . .

She slowly opened dreamy eyes
her long blond hair caressed tanned thighs
with firm full breasts and satin skin -
she was the perfect mate for sin.

Above the crashing waves Jack heard
'You saved my life . . .' (her voice just *purred*)
'Please let me do something for *you* -
I'll make your *wildest* dreams come true . . .'

Butch and Babe then joined their party
Babe, Jack thought, looked *extra* tarty . . .
'Do me a favour - cut the talk -
and take Butch here for a *long* walk . . .

Sue Millward

MY GARDEN

I love my garden lush and green,
Pity it's just weeds that can be seen.
From afar a wondrous sight,
But my lovely flowers struggle for light.

I toil daily hard and long.
But why are my weeds excessively strong?
I pull them up, and dig them out,
Still they come back without a doubt.

I sew my seedlings every spring,
I await the colours summer should bring.
Alas, even if I succeed with germination,
The slugs eat the shoots with great determination.

Well! Now on my newly dug patch of ground,
The cat performs his daily function with no sound.
Could this be fertiliser in action?
No, only my cat gets any satisfaction.

After thought and resolution,
I have found a new solution.
Replace it all with crazy paving,
To use only tubs is labour saving.

Anne Livingstone

THE FIELDS

In harvest fields the stubble shows
That all the corn is carried now.
Where once a rippling ripeness stood
The gleaning pheasants pick their nervous way.

Beside the village; there along the lane;
After the fair some other signs remain,
Of those who filled the field with noise and life
Each one has gone; and some will not return.

Man grows the grain and throws the litter down,
Drinks shouts and quarrels, mates and plays.
When time is up he must be quiet,
And shadowed evening follows every day.

But then in spring, new growth, new leaves, new flowers,
New life, new sounds - new foolishness - new ends.
So, while life continues, it will be,
More days and nights than we can count as hours.

Peter Barnes

THE MANAGER

Sometimes early sometimes late
You'll find him often in a state
Dashing here and rushing there
It's all enough to lose his hair
But when it matters
Where's he gone?
No wonder now it goes so wrong
We do our best to always please
But who's the one who has the keys?

Arthur Luke

THE CANTON HEALTH CLUB

Stern face grey bearded barman he must have been a seaman
Mac with his elastic tights on, no wonder his veins are playing
up, I need some cream for my face, we hope he don't see the
gynaecologist again.

His side kick Malci one ball wonder swallowing pints of bitter
complains about gout his red face full of psoriasis again he
will never play football again, he was rubbish anyway always
talking about himself don't forget his frozen shoulder.

Heart attack Chic slowly to the bar pint of bitter Graham don't
tell me how Rangers got on I don't want my diabetes starting
again, throw him a football Gra his aching arms won't stray, Ron
wearing council green up the ilts, been to the doctors again Chic
don't start Mac off.

Nipper your lager is in not much wrong with him walks on his
toes arthritis leg council worker pension man not much to say
playing with computers all day, at least I'm working no like you
incapacity men, don't pick on Larry and Mike, Nipper.

Conservative Mike Thatcher's knickers in his hands pint of dark
Gra down the cellar again whoop whoop dive dive Maggie at it
again this poll tax we would have caught all the illegal, talk
to Larry, Mike his pockets sewn up no shame Larry don't talk about
money you know how upset Mac gets, lottery money Malci off again
politics, check the numbers I don't trust Larry, Nipper he's made
mistakes before nearly cost us a tenner, Graham shouting last
orders Larry your round sorry it's politic Malci, Larry you won the
raffle a bottle of whisky Mac's face money to money we can't win
the lottery with him, time please and you Mike two pints of dark
to drink the Canton Health Club

John Garrett

ROAD RAGE

Don't you wave your fist at me
For I can plainly see
That you're the one at fault, not me.
Most people would agree.

If I accelerate, instead of brake
It's just a mere mistake
But for you to err
Isn't really fair on me.

You're driving far too close behind
And truly blowing my mind.
Can't you see your blasted lights
Are making me near blind?

In my mirror, I can see your face
Suffused with rage.
Calm down, for goodness sake.
Last time I saw a living creature wild as you
They kept him in a cage.

Rosemary Thomson

BABY

Is it comedy on the TV?
Or being tickled in a certain place!
That really cheers me up,
And puts a big smile on my face.

Is it the antics of our cat
Whilst chasing her clockwork mouse?
Or the dog chasing the dustman
When he calls at our house?

Well these things bring a smile
But does not get me laughing
However my baby makes me howl
With laughter when I do her bathing.

Her hair lays flat, ears stick out
She splashes with all her might
Screams, then just stares wide-eyed
Oh yes, she is such a funny mite.

Paul B Potter

COWFISH

I have been introduced to
A Cowfish.
He is bright, quite polite,
Beauteous yellow, with light
Spinning fins, and two horns
To adorn his strong head.
Soft brown satin his eyes,
And so wise. I'm beguiled
By manoeuvres quite wild.
Unique this new friend
Who can flutter and bend
With intent to bewitch.
How I wish you could say
All your eyes give away
Pretty fish. Tell me how
You were misnomered 'cow'.

Pauline Hight

PREJUDICIAL PRIDE

Who has opened up that door, there is
Such a draught about my neck
Look leaves are drifting on the floor
Oh please will someone come and check
Perhaps the windows open too, yes
My hands are turning quite quite blue
Mrs Collins, Mrs Collins
What is a soul supposed to do

Who is out there ignoring me. I shall
Come myself and then you'll care
Look, yes, I leave this quite exquisite chair
Oh now my wrath I will prepare
Perhaps you would care to take the chance
To flee, indeed I do advance
Mrs Collins, Mrs Collins
Are you contented then to face my glance

Who is it then has closed the door
Swept up the leaves lay here before
Look now the sunshine dances on the tiles
Faking leaves that were here in piles!
Perhaps you think I've turned a fool
Well I'll tell you this my house I rule
Mrs Collins, Mrs Collins
How can you be so calm and cool
Ah I remember your visiting cousin Elizabeth, such a jewel
Well whomsoever swept, their secrets safe and cunningly kept
I shall return to the exquisite chair in which I slept!

Catherine Marshall

MORE LEGS

When God made man He did quite well
But there's one thing I need.
Why couldn't I have had more legs
And been a millipede?

The two I've got are always tired,
But if I'd had lots more
They wouldn't have to do so much
And wouldn't be so sore.

Then if I went and broke one leg
I wouldn't be bereft.
I doubt if I would even know
For I'd have plenty left.

Now cycling would be quite fun
I'd keep on swapping feet,
And if I ran against my friends
I'd be so hard to beat.

At football I'd show lots of skill.
The others would be vexed.
The goalie just would never know
Which foot I'd kick with next.

Perhaps you know, it's not so good
I would have much to lose,
For think of all the time I'd spend
In doing up my shoes!

John Christopher Cole

ONY ASPRIN?

Ho Jeannie, wait a meenit, I've no seen you a' day
Whit's that? You've got a sair heid an it winna go away
You're jist oot fir a message afore you make the tea
Hud on a bit, I'll walk wi you, noo dinna rush away

Oor Tam had wan o thaie sair heids the other day you ken
He said he couldnae go tae work, he caed it a mee-grain
I caed it the fourteen pints he had the night afore
But I was kind and smiled at him as I helped him oot the door

Look, there's that wummin ower there, you ken the wan I mean
Wi spindly heels, peroxide hair, thinks she's a beauty queen
I hear she's got a fancy for thon man at number ten
If his wife finds oot, without a doot, you'll no see her again

See there's auld Peggy doon the road, is it no a cryin shame?
Fair crippled wi her corns she is, you'd think that she was lame
That's whit comes o wearin spindly heels, she should tell that ither wan
She'd be better wearin baffies and forgettin that wee man

An there's thon Wullie at his door, he's jist a fair disgrace
Stottin drunk, an it's only four, fallin a' ower the place
He's knocked that dustbin ower twice, look he's talkin tae the cat
Noo he's pit his key in upside doon, hiv you seen the likes o that?

You watch that po-faced cow in the corner shop, she wouldnae gie me tick
She thinks she's somethin special but she jist makes me sick
Nae wunner she's got money, the cost o things in there
You watch whit she charges Jeannie, noo mind an you take care

Well whit did you get fir your man's tea? Did you buy a bit o ham?
I've fish fingers fir the weans an sausages fir Tam
I'll no bother havin nuthin for I've bingo on the night
And we get fish suppers efter, so that does me a' right

Well I'd better get a move on, has your headache gone away?
Whit's that? It's even worse noo, och Jeannie you don't say
I wis thinkin you were awfy quiet, get hame and go tae bed
And let your man get his ain tea and you nurse your sair head

Gail Morgan

THE ROOM

'Do you really like to live in a tip?'
I ask my teenage son.
Dead sandwiches and evil socks,
Even a mouldy bun.

Perhaps I'll venture in today,
Perhaps I'll take a broom.
It's not the jungle I'm going in,
Just my dear son's room.

Please Keep Out, the notice says,
So I feel I must desist.
But I might pop in with this black bag,
And dust . . . just a flick of the wrist.

You've moved *my stuff!* I hear him cry,
And the echoes creep on in.
And I hear myself at sweet sixteen,
Now it's me who's committed the sin.

I know it drives me crazy, the chaos and the dirt.
But then, one day, all will be neat,
And *that* will *really hurt!*

Dot Lupo

LEGAL LIMERICK

There was a Solicitor from Devon,
Had secretaries sent from heaven.
They were prompt and polite
And incredibly bright
And they never went home before seven

They worked all day in their inimitable way,
Without a gossip or moan,
And they *never* chewed gum
Or glanced at your bum
Or stuttered at the end of a phone

This was sadly a dream
As in fact it would seem
The reverse was nearer the truth -
They lacked instant recall,
Response was a shortfall
And both were well past their youth

I don't mind I suppose,
Thought he in repose,
If they lack a certain finesse.
They put up with my muddle,
They're good for a cuddle
And impressed by my sporting prowess

Tragically sipping his tea,
He had to agree,
His wife was right all along -
I'm too soft by half,
Only good for a laugh
And I've been in the job too long.
Yes! I've been in the job too long!

Sandra Kershaw

A FUNNY FEELING

I've got a funny feeling,
It's running round my head,
I think I'm going down with something,
It's time to go to bed.

It's a feeling quite perqulia,
And it's rather unique,
It's almost as if someone,
Is kissing both my feet.

It comes from down below,
And works its way up high,
I can't take it any more,
I think I'm going to cry.

It happens quite a lot,
Oh what can I do,
I hope it's going to stop,
It makes me want the loo.

It makes my body shake,
And my face tends to stick,
My tummy starts to ache,
But I don't feel sick.

If you've ever had this feeling,
I think it's true to say,
That every human being,
Laughs in this way.

So if you feel like laughing,
Remember what to do,
You can laugh till you're crying,
But don't go far from the loo.

Kimberley Hall

HOW I SEE GOD

I see God as a double bass,
Long and deep in the face.
Black, white, whatever race,
He made the earth at His own pace.

I see God as a bag of nuts,
All around the earth as such.
People say He's all around,
Drifts past us without a sound.

I see God as a celebrity,
Damon Hill or Chris Barrie.
Nigel Planer or Rik Mayall,
A can of Coke up for sale.

I see God as a warning sign,
On a buoy floating down the Tyne.
'You'll go to heaven' He will tell,
Unlike Satanists who go to hell.

I see God as a football team,
Above the rest it may seem.
All the records He can hold,
That's because He made the world.

Jordan Evans (12)

A RABBIT DREAMS

'Thought I'd catch a rabbit,' said the farmer to his wife,
'Thought we'd have it for our dinner', and handed her the knife.
'Thought a nice fur coat, out of its skin I'd make,
Thought I'd wear it when I go fishing, down at the lake.
Thought we'd invite the neighbours over, for a bite to eat,
Thought you'd serve them rabbit stew, it would be a treat.'

'Thought I'd better tell you something,' said the wife on his return,
'Thought I'd say you've got it wrong and you really ought to learn.
Thought it time I became a cannibal and ate only human meat,
Thought Sainsbury's would sell it, but their range they had to delete.
Thought of adding broccoli florets and slops from the sty,
Thought you wouldn't mind obliging, for we're having Farmer's Pie.'

D M Wrayton

NASAL APPRAISAL

They rest so proudly in the middle of one's face,
Many Eskimos use them to meet and embrace.
They come in sizes long and small,
The largest one I've yet to recall.
Taken for granted, despicably used,
Pushed and poked, thoroughly abused.
Red and shining, wet or cold,
Covered in hairs or completely bald.
Some look like dad's and some like mum,
With a lifetime guarantee they come.
One uses them in many ways,
To smell the flowers grown on byways.

Seeking out freshly baked cakes and bread,
A detector of bacon wakes you from bed.
It has its uses for danger too,
And can warn of fire before you do.
Allergic to dust and household mite,
Sneezing continuously through the night.
This thing on one's face now taken charge,
With enormous power it looks so large.
They can fall in love I'm told at first sight.
Their not just usable, but extremely bright.
As I stand by the mirror and take a peep,
Mine looks second-hand and very cheap.

Olive Weller

WHAT'S IT ALL WORTH?

You work all your life - if you can find a job,
You buy a house - if you're lucky,
And maybe a car,
And all you've got to show at the end of the day
are wrinkles and scars.

Stress is part of everyday living,
Your mind and body being pushed to the limits,
And when old age dawns (peace) you've got a problem
with your heart,
Who wants to live to be an old fart?

So before you enjoy life it's over,
Vanished into thin air,
If life's what you make it - supposedly good,
Then there must be a lot of charlatans out there.

Carl Bridgman

THE MANY GUISES OF LAUGHTER

It's ages since I last had a good
laugh, I've had a short laugh yes, but a
long laugh, a laugh comes out of a hole in your
face, anywhere else and you're in trouble.
A laugh has many disguises
be it a smirk, giggle or belly.
It's sometimes considered 'canned' when on the telly.
Laugh and the whole world laughs with you, weep and
you weep alone, the old saying goes,
but why also that old saying 'cry yourself laughing'?
I've pondered and pondered that question, but no one knows,
but up until then I will try to cry until I end up
laughing.

A P Regan

BROTHERS

Brothers are pests
Brothers are pains
They drive you crazy
They drive you insane

They make stupid noises
And pull weird faces
You wish you could banish them
To far-off places

For their table manners
They deserve a bashin'
Rammin' it in
Like it's going out of fashion

Their habits are obscene
Not very good
Involve farting and burping
And things equally rude

They pick their noses
They scratch their bum
It proves the fact
That they're really dumb

If you don't have brothers
You're doing just fine
I've got two
So you can have one of mine!

Gillian Snaith

FISHERMAN'S NIGHTMARE

When I was a lad,
My sea shimmered,
Turquoise silver.
Now I'm older,
My sea,
Has turned a musty green.

Upon the musty green,
We discovered,
New types of fish.
Fish netted in,
Fish with two tails,
Fish with two heads.

Government officials,
Comment - well done lads!
You've discovered,
Two new species of fish.
Five miles out,
My sea turned yellow,
Each white horse,
Gallops with fested smell.

The stench of humanity,
Hangs heavy upon my bow,
Stinging my lungs,
As I vomit.
My seas have turned red,
Then emptied,
Of all its fish.

Then filled up with atomic waste,
Then capped with billions,
Of tons of sticky black.
I've noticed how,
The carbon monoxide,
Just catches our sky.

Now I have,
My own,
Northern lights
Please! Just turn,
Back the clock,
Just give me,
Back the sun.

So I,
May swim,
In blue seas,
Once again.

James Stewart

ZOE THE ZEBRA

Zoe the Zebra was feeling quite blue,
alone in her paddock with nothing to do;
fed up with people who just stood and stared,
she longed for a friend, for someone who cared.
Along came her keeper who brought her some hay,
a miserable fellow, with not much to say;
he crossed to the manger, then realised too late,
he'd forgotten to slip the catch on the gate.
Quick as a flash our young Zoe was out;
the keeper could only just manage to shout;
she flew through the exit galloping fast,
so happy at finding her freedom at last.
at the end of the lane, leaning over a wall,
was a large white bull, nearly six foot tall.
Zoe slowed down, and with eyelashes fluttering,
'For a living,' she asked, 'just what do you do?'
And the bull looked her up and down, and said,
'Get those pyjamas off, and I'll show you.'

David T Wicking

IN THE MOOD

I grappled with grinning crocodile
In fathomless murky deep;
. . . Ran a blistering twenty-mile marathon -
Scaled slippery slopes in my sleep.

I tickled a tiger till its stripes fell off,
In a jungle tangled with snakes;
. . . Bungi-jumped dressed up as a cockerel -
Scoffed one hundred and ten fresh cream cakes.

I hen-pecked a parrot to distraction,
Pretty Polly my persistent phrase;
. . . Flew to Barbados minus Jumbo jet -
It just happened to be one of those days.

Christina Angelique

MONDAY MORNING

The alarm goes off at six once more,
I fall out of bed and onto the floor.
Burning the toast and dropping the jam,
Makes me realise how sleepy I am.
I grab my briefcase and trip over the cat,
Get in the car but the battery's flat.
I ring for a taxi but there isn't one free,
I'm late to the office, everyone's there except me.
I press the button but the lift won't work,
I hear it coming, then it stops with a jerk.
I run up the stairs past ten other floors,
Get to my office and burst through the doors.
I've got twenty-five clients waiting at my desk,
I hunt through my files but they're all in a mess.
It's only 11.30 and I'm already yawning,
But then it's always like this - on a Monday morning.

Kirsti Ansell

GUNGIE

After the telephone message came,
Life could never be the same again
One or our friends had gone away
But forever in our thoughts will stay.

I remember holidays by the sea,
First there, rubbing his hands with glee.
A man respected, loved and admired.
With virtues not every man acquired.

He left behind his children and wife,
The most important things in his life.
He would be proud of his girls all three,
And a grandad now he'd be.

His daughter's wedding, his wife took his place,
I felt a tear, run down my face.
My friend I know she misses him still,
And in her heart she always will.

Pat Fitton

INVENTOR OF MIME!

Since I was taught at the village school
More than sixty years have passed,
I won't say they were the happiest days of my life,
Although I liked English and maths.
But because I can't sing a note in tune,
When it came to music time
I formed the words but made no sound,
Was I the inventor of mime?

Ivy Neville

TO SNEEZE OR WHEEZE

Oh, let's get rid of the dreadful sneeze,
The thing that makes humans begin to wheeze.
It's really quite silly and awfully tedious,
Well, I mean, choking and spluttering,
When you're trying to look serious.
It can't be done gracefully and certainly not quietly,
It just comes right out, in its mind-bending entirety.
I really have practised, secretly quite hard,
Learning how to sneeze, so as not to cause alarm.
But I'm sorry when it comes,
There's no holding back,
And those who are near, come under attack.

Carolyn Kirk

LIVING AND DYING

Life must have a reason for us to live and die
Like why is just a reason for us to reason why
To die is not to live and to live is not to die
Which is true of someone living and they certainly won't deny
But to someone who has lived and now has passed away
Cannot be in agreement because they're not here to say
Yet if someone had asked them when they were here to live
Would have said I'm not dead yet so no answer can I give
Now I apologise to all the dead who may have read this with laughter
But maybe some of the living will before joining the hereafter
So take all the time to laugh and all the time to cry
And really enjoy your living before it's your time to die
Then if you should find you can't afford the funeral expense
Just go on with your living that's surely common sense.

F E Wentworth

DEATH'S HEAD HAWK

Do you really want to have a laugh,
At me, when I fell out of the bath.
I was draped half on the floor,
My feet in the bath, my head hit the door.
O dear! What a start to the day,
I thought to myself, as I lie in this way.
I knew I'd put in too much stuff,
I'd emptied the lot, there was enough,
Lying there, pampering myself,
Adding more bath oil off the shelf
Tipping in fragrances, of lemons and lime,
Whilst I was turning into a mass of slime.
Well I was alright 'til I saw the moth,
That flew from out of the pink face cloth,
Aaaaaa! It's flying straight for me,
It's at that point I tried to flee,
My legs did not go in the same direction,
Flapping my arms to give me protection.
My eyes were fixed on the moth with a stare,
'Twas at that point I was in mid-air
It was huge, enormous, as big as a bat.
You'd think that if you were half on the mat
Where is it now? Have those wings got stuck?
It's flown out the window, what a stroke of luck!
What a state of the place, suds everywhere,
Oil on the floor, slime in my hair.
I rise gracefully, slower than when I went down
My face adorning a very big frown,
A knock at the door (my husband), are you alright flower?
Yes thanks, I'm fine I'm having . . . a shower!

Dawn Ridler

THE WAKE OF THE BURN

The damming of great rivers
For hydro-powered schemes
Meander not of nature
But, by dynamite it seems
Safe from such fate
The little burn
With trout to suit its size
Not so, a mighty blast upstream
I witnessed its demise.

Seems it overflowed at times
Into adjoining fields
Bought by a new farmer
Stern priority in yields
One stretch, a boisterous rapids
Their loud bickerings
I held dear
Watery voices in death throes
That day, came to my ear.

As twilight cast a shroud
I stepped unto the blackened bed
Foot resting on, a slime-clad rock
In sadness bowed, my head
Reborn of new direction
In canal way, to a 'mere'
I bid adieu
Wee burn I knew
And loved of yesteryear.

Liam McKinney

THE SOFA SPUD

My husband's a Couch Potato.
Does nothing else but watch sport.
With a winning bet, got a TV set.
Says the very best thing he's bought.

His eyes it would seem are turning square.
Like some sort of television infection.
He'll eat, he'll drink without even a blink.
Nor changing his gaze of direction.

In his mind he's wherever the match is.
Imagining he'll be called to play.
He made so much noise being one of the boys.
That our neighbours have moved far away.

Even the call of nature must wait.
For the break; this is him being rash.
Then it's sprint to the loo like a bolt from the blue.
A world record, this twenty foot dash.

Who notices the 'food and watering' person?
I've even tried wearing disguises.
Mind, he did go quite red, when I loudly said.
'It's all balls. Different shapes, different sizes.'

There's a snooker tournament approaching.
I'll be brushing my teeth till they're pearly.
Next I'm packing my bag, what's more, taking the 'Jag'.
Then I'm off, for my holidays, early.

Violette Edwards

WAITING FOR A TRAIN

I've been late before.
Waited for a train
before,
waiting to be late.
I've sat here
and watched the rain
or winter pressing down.
I've seen the sunlight
sparkling cars
in buoyant spring.
Then, high summer hot,
watched the heat in layers
simmer from the ground.
I've been here
so many times
waiting
to work
to play
to share
to go away.

Helen Lovelock Burke

UN-TITLED

I saw some throttle cable
    In my local Oxfam shop
And wondered who to throttle
    Who I'd like to chop.

I could visualise the headlines
    VAT man RIP
Unknown assailant strikes again
    It's bye-bye TSB.

I would love to knock the block off
        My accountant and all suits;
Thatcher-Murdoch-Bottomley,
        I'd fell them in their boots.

But I said 'I'd like the cable
        For my yellow 2CV.'
Only when I came to pay I found
        I'd lost the 50p.

Sarah Lidell

SPIRIT LEVEL

I want to lift my spirits
        (preferably with gin)
Not feel so stern and dour
        dabble in some 'sin'
Erase the frown and glower
        replace it with glitz

I want to have a 'happy hour'
        (gimme a rum and coke)
maybe trip the light fantastic
        where do I find a bloke?
To get out there and frolic
        what if it turns sour?

My spirits now are sinking fast
        (I need a double brandy)
How can I keep my chin up
        preferably all three?
I think it's easier to sit and sup
        and (s)wallow in the past

        Just fill up my glass

Margaret Sturgess

A MOVING STORY

I've just got home, my love has gone,
The house is cleared I see.
Has she run off with a moving man,
And left me with no tea?

Well nuts to her, I just don't care;
Good riddance, 'on yer bike'.
I'll find another girl friend,
Maybe one I'll even like.

I mean, she was no beauty,
And looked just like her mother,
With sharp eyes so untrusting,
That they closely watched each other.

Still, I've no claim to good looks,
And I've suffered from the mockers.
One even used my likeness
As a model for door knockers.

My wavy hair has waved goodbye,
My seat is sadly sagging.
My 'get up and go' has 'got up and gone'
And my energy is flagging.

So honestly, we made a pair,
Proclaiming love so hammily.
Not quite the stuff of Mills and Boon -
More like the Addams Family.

But, hark, it's the telephone, it's her;
I've been thoroughly reproved.
I know I'm a fool, but I'll tell you,
I'd completely forgotten - we've moved.

James Bell

TO BSE OR NOT TO BSE?

Beef's off the menu I suddenly declared,
So some disease that we can be spared.
Husband he moaned, 'cos he's partial to steak,
Taken to beef, like a duck to a drake!
All of a sudden I was truly inspired,
Bought all the ingredients my heart desired.
But the spaghetti looked lonely laid there all bare,
It isn't the same when the sauce isn't there!
I tried to get better with my next dish,
Off to the chip shop and bought him a fish!
Then I tried harder and made him a stew,
But he searched for the meat for an hour or two!
I started to worry that he'd start losing weight,
Or perhaps he'd clear off and find a new mate!
So off on my travels I started again,
Cursing all cows and one or two men!
Found what I wanted; a new cookery book;
Hoping this time that I'd have better luck.
I spent quite some time as I chopped and I stirred,
Grated and strained as the processor whirred.
Time soon sped by and I knew he was late,
I thought he'd succumbed to a terrible fate,
At last he came home and then said to me,
None for me dear, I've just had my tea!
My anger rose quickly, my face it turned pink,
He cottoned on quickly, and before he could think,
I'd lifted the bin and tipped his tea inside,
Then turned to him quickly but slowly replied,
I've wasted my time dear, and then so have you,
'Cos I've left lots of pots for you to do!

C A Danby

LAUGHTER - THE KEY!

Many a laugh I have had
Many a tear been shared.
Laughter is a good, fun thing
Which should be shared
Between two or more friends.
Laughter makes you cheerful
And willing to share.
Share a joke with a friend
Rather than an argument
With some stranger.
Have a laugh, don't be a bore!

Share a joke in the pub with a mate,
Make somebody's day be being the fool
Give somebody else a laugh if one can't.
Laughter is nicer to see
Than brawling and fighting.
Don't be a fool have a laugh.

Laughter can be due to a joke,
A fool, an act, somebody messing around
Or even because you are happy and cheerful.
Laughter can occur because of embarrassment
A way to hide the shame of one.
Laughter can be because one is excited.

What other way can you think of
To show excitement and enjoyment?
Tears. They often show happiness,
Yet they look as sad.
Some are drunk who laugh and giggle
Some laugh at another or the way they laugh.
Laughter should be shared - have a laugh and a giggle!

Samantha Malster

MEN IN THE KITCHEN

Rice in the kettle
Veg soaked in Dettol,
Dirties in the dryer
Ice-cream in the fryer.
Who'd have a man in the kitchen?
Ironing in the washer
Tea stains on me jotter,
Cornflakes in the freezer,
'Cor blimey' what a geezer.
Who'd have a man in the kitchen?
Lettuce on the boil
Covered in garden soil,
Jelly in the microwave,
Not another midnight rave!
Who'd have a man in the kitchen?
Beer bottles everywhere,
He doesn't even seem to care,
Is he still drunk?
What a skunk,
What happened to my handsome hunk?
Me vows that I swore,
Till death do us part,
I'll have to swap him
In the Exchange and Mart.
'Does anybody want my man?'
I'll gladly exchange him
With a rusty old van,
But don't ring too late
Because I can't wait,
Who'd have me man in their kitchen?

Stephanie Hall

CHOOSING YOUR MAN

Strike, while the iron is hot
Is a phrase, my mother used a lot
Do everything, that you possibly can
Go out there, and get your man!
Whatever colour, black or white
Even if, he's a hideous sight
Be sure, that, he lives on his own
Has a sporting car, and a mobile phone.
I only want, the best for you
Single rich men, are very few
Marry a doctor, or a millionaire
I promise you'll make, the perfect pair.
Materialistic, is how I sound
When I say, money makes the world go round
But I am, a lot older than you
And am well aware, of what is true.
With money, you can do anything
Happiness, is what money can bring.

Shabnam Walji

YOU MAKE ME LAUGH AUNTY TRACEY!

You make me laugh Aunty Tracey
You tickle me pink
With your crazy but funny ways
You really make me smile

I can remember one afternoon
When we went on a children's ride
It went slow, you fell down
And fell on your backside.

I can remember your fear of snakes
When we went to Chester Zoo
When my dad moved the hosepipe you thought it was a snake
I thought you were going to faint.

You have done some funny things
You really make me laugh
Although you sometimes embarrass me
I love you to bits.

Sarah Jones-Davies (11)

GARDENER'S QUESTION TIME

Can someone please explain to me
Why it should be so,
That the seeds I plant with loving care
Never seem to grow?
Yet weeds grow in abundance
They spring up with great vigour
Even when I dig them up
They simply grow back bigger.

Buttercup and dandelion,
Nettles by the score,
Clover, vetch and bindweed,
And several dozen more
All will flourish happily
Sans love, sans help, sans care
Unlike the plants I've nurtured.
It seems a bit unfair.

But I think I've found the answer
Because I've bought this pack of seeds
To grow a wildlife garden
It's a garden full of weeds.

Anne Brennan

JONES THE 'PHONE

Once there was a man called Jones,
Who imitated the ringing 'phone.
The excellence of his emulation
Caused his friends much frustration.
In every direction they would be
Seeking a hand-set they couldn't see.
Jones would further infuriate all,
Seriously pretending to answer the call.
He would listen with affected air,
Then shrug and say, 'There's nobody there.'
Poor Jones, one day emitted the sound,
Theatrically answered - then fell to the ground.
Never again did he try that joke,
He swore someone answered when he spoke.

Bernard Curtis

WHEN YOU'VE BEEN DUMPED!

He said goodbye - 'See ya, old gal!'
He's dumped ya for your best pal
you go to bed, you lie awake
girl, give yourself a break
sit down with the old CD's
and droll over Keanu Reeves
forget the sucker and his attitude
you're entitled to your mood
don't worry about your tum
or what he thinks about your bum!
Squeeze yer big, fat juicey spots
that are bigger than jelly tots
flirt with that guy like crazy
don't worry about being lazy
laugh aloud when he walks by.

Lakshmi Agrawal

THE DASHING WHITE DENTIST

Famous abroad for his charm and finesse,
His skill with a drill is a roaring success,
With a scale or a polish, a bridge or a crown
This angel in white will banish your frown.

Children all love his smiles and his jokes,
No need for parents to comfort or coax,
Never was any child ever so willing to
Go for a check-up, a brace, or a filling
Sitting agog at the ceiling they stare
At favourite videos - all are there,
Batman, Superman Thunderbirds II,
Robin Hood, Turtles, Star Trek and crew,
And when it's all over the nurse, who's so jolly
Gives them a treat, like a toy or a lolly.

Under his gaze the ladies all swoon
Regular visits can't come too soon,
'Come in, my dear, would you like to sit there?'
('For you, darling doctor, we'd sit anywhere!')
'No sweeties, no toffees, just lots of good brushing'
'Whatever you say!' they murmur, all flushing
But when they get home it's all sugar and cake,
Anything that will give them tooth-ache,
A few weeks go by, and they phone, sounding sad,
'Oh dear, it's my tooth, I'm afraid that it's bad;
It's such hard luck but I think Heaven sent it,
I'll have to revisit my dashing white dentist!'

Ruth Callan

MY SON'S BIKE

A bike is what he's nagged for
Over the past two years or three!
Dreams of riding down the motorway
At speeds of one hundred and three.

He sits astride this monster tank
His helmet's all askew.
His legs drag on the tarmac
Too tall! A thing I always knew.

He has to push to start it
The damp's got in you see.
The exhaust does blow - I'm not surprised.
It's nearly forty three!

He wanted something special
Something good and spanking new!
But to get this from the scrapyard
I even had to queue!

He's good at all mechanics
Or so he says he's keen.
Let's see if he can change it
Into his dream machine!

Linda Somner

BUNDLE OF JOY

Swollen ankles, puffy legs,
Sudden cravings for raw eggs,
For nine long months I waddled around,
My belly almost touching the ground.

It wriggles and kicks, it feels like a team,
By the end of it all, I'm sure I will scream,
I'm marking the calendar day by day,
When my waters break, I'm on my way.

The fateful day has finally arrived,
How on earth have I survived?
Now I am panting, so any time now,
I'm about to give birth, it feels like ahhh cow!

One last push, and the end is in sight,
It's nearly all over, must get it just right,
It isn't a girl, so it must be a boy,
Now I am cuddling my bundle of joy.

Susan May Downs

THE PULTENEY ARMS

He pays for his drink and props up the bar,
He left his brain behind in the car.
His mates are there, his girlfriend's hair,
Falls graceful in the smoky air.

The usual looks, surveillance cool,
Then lips back to the one pint pool.
The endless chatter dips and dives,
And soon his thought's anaesthetised.

Another order, another round,
And he feels lighter by a few more pounds.
And soon the room begins to sway,
The dull lights bend diagonal rays.

And faces blurred like frosted glass,
He sees his stomach walking past.
So out the door he follows it,
They walk behind, with faces lit

By black blue skies, they tumble out,
To end the night in wordless shouts.

Stephen Nicholas

DEAR MR JONES

I am so sorry Mr Jones, my mind went blank,
forgot the appointment at the bank.
Can I arrange another date?
Promise this time I won't be late.

Mr Jones I know I owe so much,
but I know you will always keep in touch,
the letters you sent me are under the bed,
you always seem lately to write them in red.

Never mind, cheer up, it's not so bad.
Owing you money won't make me sad,
after all it can only get better,
and you never fail to send me a letter.

What are these fees you say I owe?
I thought my money had started to grow,
I counted the figures all in black,
thought I had made quite a stack!

I will meet you next week, at quarter to four,
I know your office your name's on the door,
you know I will always be loyal and true,
then your letters to me can be written in blue.

Lynne Mair Iles

THE GENTLE SLOB

'Here comes Harry they cried, pour him another gin;
And relieve him of his coat, (refused by every bin.)
'When you poke fun at his sewer like stench,
Harry won't mind, he'll take it on the chin.'

Harry (Ginger) Yates, president elect of drink;
Known by every man, he's spewed in every sink.
Mock Harry, mock Harry, Harry 'the slob' won't mind,
But in Harry the man, you'll never perceive a chink.

Harry, dear Harry what mess does your soul hide beneath?
Do you remember that night, when struck by a foolish thief?
He could not believe the ghoul he stood before
And fled along the road, vilified in grief.

Now when your flame dims and you hear the last stop tap
And fear grips the face of every solemn chap:
Think not of their torment and ever lasting despair;
But give a happy cheer Harry, for the end of all that c--p!

Stephen Cantello

U F O

(A dedication to Mandi)

Have you fairies at the bottom of your garden
There's a space ship at the bottom of mine
I often go to have a look when I have the time.

The spacemen aren't green as you might think
Actually they're a lovely shade of pink
They don't have antennae coming from their noses
Their pink is the pink of my best roses

There could be three of them or maybe four
As when I try to count them, they slam the spaceship door
They've got star shaped heads all glowing and bright
That turn on and off according to the light

They seem to have ten legs or more
That somehow don't quite reach the floor
Their names must be finkle, as that's all they ever say
Whether I'm listening at night, or in the day.

They arrived on Thursday at three in the afternoon
They've been here six months, so they could be going soon
I can't invite you to come and see
As they're only here especially for me.

Pat Grogan

THE FROG'S LAMENT

As I sat on me lily pad and croaked me froggy song,
And feasted on some passing flies a princess came along.

She looked at me with careworn eyes, 'Oh little frog,' she said,
'There are no handsome princes left. They've all got up and fled.'

'An ancient witch, in ancient days,' she went on to explain,
'Had cursed them with an aweful curse and they would not remain.'

I croaked a little froggy croak, which could have been translated
As, 'I'm a prince who has been cursed and to a frog mutated.'

'I have been doomed to spend my time as an amphibian
Until a princess kisses me, when I'll become a man.'

The princess did not understand, but still she picked me up.
'Oh frog,' she said, 'you're very cute.' And I responded, 'Glupp.'

She ran her fingers down my back, and stroked my slimy chin,
And closed her eyes, and pursed her lips, and I thought, 'Frog. You're in.'

She held me gently on her breast, caressed me with her hand
And squeezed me where she shouldn't have, which I found rather grand.

She sniffed me with a gentle sniff, and then she said to me,
'I'm glad you're here 'cos now I'll have some frog's legs for my tea.'

Ian Ashton

MAX

Have you ever bathed a hamster?
That's a job and a half.
We had to use a toothbrush
And a little tub once used for Marge.

The shampoo cleaned the soot off
We dare not touch your face
We couldn't bear to frighten you
Once you were rescued from the fire place.

You looked so sad and dejected
A wet and scrawny thing
But that did not deter you
Or make you regret the little fling

Its unbelievable how we dried him
We set the hair dryer on cool
It must be the first time a hamster had a blow dry
While washing his face and keeping his
Whiskers in trim.

Elizabeth Amery

THE NIGHT SHIFT

I've won the pools
It's quite a bit
My record is a massive hit
I get my first Oscar today
My show's the toast of old Broadway
My jet awaits to fly to Cannes
I'm dining with the Aga-Kagn
I've been to the palace, once or twice,
The president rings for my advice.
I am the heart of every social scene
In every country I have been
I have more homes, than you have clocks
My yacht awaits in its own dry docks.
Here I stand in my penthouse suite
Survey - The world beneath my feet
And as I turned to walk away
A voice from far-away did say
'Its time you looked out for a life
            or you'll be late to start your shift'

Francis John Law

PAST TIMES

Those bygone years that stay in your brain
Are ones you'll never live again
Like childhood memories now long past
A time you thought wouldn't go fast
Becoming a teenager you can remember that part
The romances and idols that stole your heart
After that an adult you've become
With a few tears but mostly fun
Choosing a partner and planning your wedding day
Those memories will never fade away
Then you recall those babes in their cots
And the love and fun of those tiny tots
Those past years with happy scenes
When your children reached their teens
All those years are in the past
But the memory will always last
You look at the photos and to yourself say
It only seems like yesterday.

Merril Morgan

TRICKLING WATERS

When I go for petrol I always want a wee,
I think I've got a problem from drinking too much tea,
As petrol starts to flow, I start to wriggle round,
And as I try to hold it, there's not a dry eye in the crowd,
You think your feeling better till you hit the bumpy road,
Then it gets much worse and your going to explode,
I'm sitting at the traffic lights just about to scream,
But as it starts to trickle out, they have gone to green,
I'm jumping up and down now, fighting with my zipper,
Feeling warm and wet now, I wish that I'd been quicker.

Elizabeth T Lovis

HEADLINE NEWS

I booked in to have a new hair-do
To try to create the new me.
They told me that Sue
Was off with the 'flu
But their newest girl Donna was free.

Now no-one can say that I'm prudish
For I'd be the last to condemn
But I have to report
Donna's skirt was so short
That it only had room for the hem.

I didn't much care for her manner.
Her styling ideas made me cringe.
She told me my hair
Was much too severe
And cut me an uneven fringe.

With a huge nylon cape she encased me.
I told her ' Tight curls I detest'
So it fair made me squirm
When she gave me a perm
And my arms were not free to protest.

Dyeing my hair was disastrous.
She said that she hoped I would like
It luminous green
And at least I'd be seen
When out in the dark on my bike.

I certainly changed my whole image
There's no way I can dispute that.
Now I only go out
When there's no-one about
And then when I'm wearing a hat.

Jean Back

A LITTLE BIRD

The little bird sits in a tree
Twittering away so merrily
I hear it mostly everyday
Every time I pass that way
Its songs ringing out so clearly
In my heart I hold it dearly
Its lovely voice so full of love
As it sings in that tree above
I know you think that it's absurd
I used to love that little bird
But one day twittering with glee
The dirty little bugger shit on me.

David Brownley

WATCHING BIRDS

My husband is a twitcher.
His whoring is frequent,
At the side of quiet roads,
And in bushes, and up trees.

The birds he ogles are
Red-breasted, Blue-titted,
Ash-coloured, Black-necked,
Common, Cuddy,
Glossy goat suckers,
Gor Maws, Harriers,
Hooded, Horny,
Kittwakes, Langy,
Sand Larks, Scarbers,
Wheeties, White Rumps,
Fuckwinds, Yogles;
I hate them all.

I wish I'd never noticed
That vivid golden oriel
Out walking together
In the honeymoon light.

Lisa Kiew

BODY BUILDING

I need an extra pair of hands
I'll put them on my head.
I could comb my hair while driving,
or knit while, I'm in bed.

I need an eye to see more things,
I'd put that on my finger.
That's good, but when I wash
I'd have to watch out where it lingers.

I definitely need a better brain,
I could put it in a pocket,
and when I need to think a lot
I could plug it in a socket.

Now what about a nice new nose,
I could turn it up-side down.
So I don't smell my onion breath,
but in rain I might well drown.

My feet are wrong, I don't need them
It's wheels that I would take,
Great, I'd whizz along all day,
But where to put thc brake?

J Jones

OH! TO BE SLIM

One day I decided I was fat!
And this was this, and that was that,
I went down to the local pub,
And there I joined a slimming club.

I went upstairs where there I paid,
And then was told, to get weighed,
I must've weighed - oh half a ton!
My battle with food had just begun.

I sat and listened with great joy,
To others, who seemed to share my ploy,
For my love of eating, and for food,
I went home in a better mood.

I starved myself for seven days,
So that I, would deserve the praise,
For the pounds and inches, I had lost,
And never minded about the cost!

And so, I wanted to be slim,
And attractive, size 12 and trim,
And so from food - I must refrain,
I never want to be *Fat* again.

Sue Butcher

ORPHEUS IN HIS UNDERWEAR

In the arid air of the evening in the Great Australian Bight,
They like a little music to prepare them for the night;
And hairy Harry Barry in his sweaty cotton vest
Enmouths his penny whistle, and inflates his tattooed chest,
And he blows a shrivelled squeak, and a damply dribbled moan,
And he takes a swig of Fosters, and he spits upon a stone;
And again he points his whistle at the pale, sardonic moon,
And he purples like a plum in his passion for a tune.
But he doesn't have it in him, and he never gets it right,
And the people starve for melody, night after flaming night.
But they have a local legend, of a Pentecostal eve,
When he blew a run of crochets, and a thoughtful semi-breve
In the key of C sharp minor, and some clear augmented thirds,
And a strong diminished seventh, with a cadence like a bird's.
And for twenty magic seconds the music of the spheres
Rang round the crimson caverns of their hairy Ossy ears.
But the tongues of flame departed, and they never came again,
And the empty tubes of Fosters pile round the yard in vain.

The folk are quite progressive on the South Australian shore.
They've got a dozen bar rooms, and they're building several more.
They've got a roller skating rink, and bingo hall as well,
And a little supermarket, and a small one-star hotel.
They're thinking of a bioscope and modest local zoo;
But they'll never make a Glyndebourne out of Gungeridgiddoo.

K D Savell

QUIET PLEASE

'Get into a book'
My teacher said,
So me and my mates quickly sped,
To the back of the library,
Where we sat and read.

The teacher watched us,
Like a hawk does its prey,
One false move,
And she'll be here right away.

We read for a while,
But that wasn't our style,
The temptation grew,
And the teacher was new.

It started with a whisper,
Then a giggle
Before I knew it
I had stitches in my middle.

I tried to control it,
But I just couldn't stop,
She caught me red handed,
And she was off.

Shouting and screaming
Things at me,
I looked desperately for an escape,
But she'd had her meal and now I was her cake.

Abigail Hughes (13)

DIET DILEMMA

All those things you mustn't eat
Keep them for that special treat,
Chicken supreme
With real dairy cream,
Bacon 'n egg
For that you beg,
Custard trifle
The need you stifle.
I know these goodies I'm denied
Roasted spuds and chips deep fried,
Not only do they block the ticker
But make my waistline clearly thicker,
Those tasty foods I must resist
My health food book I will enlist,
Mushroom pud
I know I should,
Wholemeal bread
Now that I dread,
Lentil tart
That makes me fart,
Maybe if the two are blended
My fatty diet could be mended,
Oven chips
I'll get to grips,
Bangers grilled
I'm not so thrilled,
Cream-less cake
An effort I'll make,
OK I'll give it a stab
Occasionally sneaking a Donna Kebab.

Pauline Jones

A LANDLORD'S TALE

Big Duggy from Denny, he thought he was fly,
Smuggling moonshine into the bar;
'This'll do us the night boys, nae need to buy,
Just the one so's to get us a jar,'
'What's that ye've got there?', 'It's fae Bobby McNair,
It's a present for doing his pipes.
It's as prickly as gorse, but it kicks like a horse,
So he says, and he's one of those types
That'll never tell lies where a bevvy's involved',
And he threw one inside with a 'Cheers!'
Through one-eighty degrees, his head it revolved
And a purple fur sprang from his ears.
And then out popped his tongue, rolling down to the floor
As it wrapped itself tight round his knees,
So no way could he move (yes, it was bloody sore)
'Oh Jesus! What's happening, God! Please!'
But God wasn't in, he was deaf to the cry,
As Duggy's backbone grew much shorter,
Back over he bent, and I'll tell you, no lie,
His language was blacker than porter.

His blue eyes bulged till he blew his fuse;
Where Duggy had stood, now stood only his shoes.

So his girlfriend was phoned, the bad news was broken;
Duggy had had one too many,
And not a few tears were shed as great things were spoken
Of that smashing big bloke from Denny.
So next time you're tempted to pour your own jar,
Think of Duggy from Denny and Nemesis;
Only drinks that are bought from behind this here bar,
May be consumed on the premises.

Donald McCracken

THE POINT OF NO RETURN

The time comes,
But it's going to be hard.
Hard to leave the most cold-blooded
of mums.

All the fights we have.
All the tears that fall.
If they ever turned to stone,
they could build a wall.

I walk down the stairs.
My life in my case.
A sight to bring sheer happiness
to her face.

My emotions start bubbling
up inside.
For once she said,
'I love you'
Oh how well she lied.

She shows me the door
Then watches me, stroll up the path.
I look round, stare into her eyes
I give her the message
they'll be no more.

No more hatred
No more fear
No more loneliness . . .
It'll all be so clear.

Lisa Randle

THE MEAT OF POLITICS

I am a Tory Minister.
I feed my children beef.
This isn't really sinister;
I do it for my chief.
For everyone's expendable
When Market Forces rule,
And Tories are dependable
When beef is sold at school.

What reason rule of market place
Or keeping business free,
If you can't risk the human race
by spreading BSE?
There's more than clubs to our reform
When beef-sale plans are ready
And though your brain be spongiform,
Donations remain steady.

Priority of businesses!
A Tory's primary function,
Carried out with just excess,
Zeal, concern and unction.
Good image is a major task
For ministers of Britain;
And, of The Media they ask
No bad reports be written.

Then British beef will be restored
to every dinner menu,
Where BSE can be ignored
In every class of venue,
That Tory fortunes elevate
And make all Britain glad
To have roast beef on every plate,
Lest others think us mad.

L Keen

LINES FINE AND A TRAFFIC WARDEN

There once was a 'bright' traffic warden,
So zealous folk shook on his yellow line,
They feared for the slip of white paper,
Tucked in their windscreen wiper they'd find.

But one particular day was his downfall,
A hearse dared to park on his yellow lines,
Inside was a body of an 100 years old woman,
A lady well past caring about his paper fines.

He had a quiet word with the undertaker,
'Normally I'd taken no action against a hearse,'
'Then why now' asked the undertaker
'Why? There's three cars with mourners and this hearse.'

What a shout, what a noise, what an uproar,
Incensed were the relations and friends,
'How dare he,' that 'bright' traffic warden,
Even the vicar added to the sermons.

Three cars with mourners and the hearse,
Parked on yellow lines outside a church,
It's now been written chapter and verse,
Of to do and gossip there's been much.

Said a Police Inspector, 'A storm in a teacup,
Nobody was booked no tickets issued. Hump!'

Betty Eileen Houghland

MY SISTER'S DILEMMA

The problem with my sister,
        Is she cannot land her man.
She's found the one she wants,
        but he doesn't understand.
She wants to spend her life with him,
        the good times warts and all.
But trying to get it through to him,
        is like talking to a brick wall.
She says she likes his little bum,
        because its cute and small.
So when she gets it through to him,
        She may land him after all.
Until this actually happens and she doesn't
                        have to dream,
Maybe she'll understand having a man isn't
                        what it seems.
They nag and moan and watch TV,
        and shout 'Oh God!' have you done my tea.
So while you wait just take a break,
        he'll come to you before its too late.

Paquita Rockley

THE PERFECT PARTNER
(LADIES DAY AT THE GOLF CLUB)

Are you sure you didn't see my ball, I made a good connection,
If I hadn't lost my balance, it might have been perfection,
I kept my head down, followed through, much to my surprise,
It's a pity that my hat slipped down and 'blinded' both my eyes.
Are you sure you didn't see my ball, I gave it such a smack,
You really think it hit that tree and passed us coming back?
We'll have to get a move on else we'll have to call them through,
Look what happened last week, another fine to-do,
You had to tell that lady that her language wasn't pretty,
I did my best to warn you that she sits on our committee.
Look, we've got two men behind us, where did they come from?
Let's make another effort else the daylight will be gone.
I know we've not been very long, (although it seems like hours)
We've only had a flask of tea and picked a few wild flowers.
I hope they don't turn nasty, you know what some are like,
Shall we give them this last pasty and pretend I lost a spike?
One of them is stretched right out, he doesn't look too good,
You don't think my ball ricocheted and felled him where he stood?
Are you sure you didn't see my ball, I know you like to lark,
Oh, please don't go and leave me, *I'm frightened of the dark.*

Pat Blackman

THE UNLOVED

A wasp may not be beautiful
And may not be very smart
But beneath that fierce exterior
There beats a loving heart

You certainly were not matey
When that one came near you
He was trying to be romantic
When you hit him with your shoe

And you whacked him with a newspaper
And squirted him with spray
If you had only smiled at him
It would have made his day

When you saw him gaily flying
To the jam that you'd just made
To give you his opinion
Whether it had made the grade

Did you have to swat him senseless
And hurl him through the door
He's just looking for affection
Not a head that's bruised and sore.

When he zoomed so closely round you
In his loving little way
Did you have to lash out wildly
When his respects he tried to pay

Perhaps you'd better think it over
And try to make amends
Or you can bet that very soon
He'll be back with all his friends.

Sylvia Hillman

BAD ADVICE

I have a tale to tell you about a creature that was scared
He lived in fear of motor cars and thought that no-one cared.
Now this animal wasn't a badger a ferret or a dog,
It was little Bert from Brambley Wood a spikey shy, hedgehog.

One day there came a rabbit who was touched by Bertie's plight
And he tried to think of anyway to help and cure his fright,
He decided to convince him crossing roads could be real fun
Completely sure that he could show just how easily it was done.
Rabbit bounded forward into the country lane
With a speeding car approaching he could soon be in great pain,
Facing the oncoming vehicle his paws in a kind of salute
The driver saw him, honked his horn, it made a loud toot-toot.

The rabbit didn't move an inch, the car it didn't swerve
As it passed right over the little beast who'd truly shown his nerve
Hopping back to the hedgerow with a smile upon his face
'And now' he said 'It's up to you to go and take my place'.

Bertie wasn't quite that sure, could he see this trick again?
Smiling rabbit understood, Berts terror it was plain
Not once or twice but three times more the rabbit performed the feat
Till all at once Bert did decide his fear he could finally beat
Some lights were fast approaching along the leafy lane
Bert crept out from his hiding place. But his effort was in vain
For as he remembered rabbits words 'It's easy just like that'
The car reached his position and there was a sickening 'Splat'

Rabbit rushed to Bertie's side and the hedgehog raised his head
As he listened quite intently to what his tutor said,
'I'm sorry little hedgehog' he sobbed through all his tears'
'But that's the first Reliant Robin that's been down this road for years!'

Stephen P Jennings

HOME FROM HOME

You could live for a month in my husband's car
should you hit a snowdrift or get lost in the mist
on the moor.
There's old socks and scarves in my husband's car
packets of crisps and nuts
so you never would starve.
But something more, there's cushions and rugs
and there on the floor in the mud and straw
is reading galore.
Sales tickets and forms, schedules for shows,
manuals for cars, cough-cure for calves
and should you need home there's a mobile phone
in my husband's car.

Muriel Reed

INFORMATION

We hope you have enjoyed reading this book - and that you will continue to enjoy it in the coming years.

If you like reading and writing poetry drop us a line, or give us a call, and we'll send you a free information pack.

Write to

Poetry Now Information
1-2 Wainman Road
Woodston
Peterborough
PE2 7BU